ALL
IN

JESUS PLUS NOTHING
EQUALS EVERYTHING

ALL IN

THE LIFE, MESSAGE, AND LEGACY

of

JOHN MAISEL

Movement Day Publishing
New York City

Movement Day Publishing is the publishing ministry of Movement.org, an organization that catalyzes leaders in more than one hundred cities to see their cities flourish spiritually and socially. Movement.org trains leaders globally to create their own Movement Day Expressions.

For more information, visit movement.org.

ALL IN: The Life, Message, and Legacy of John Maisel

Editor: Ginger Kolbaba
Copyeditor: Christy Distler
Cover design: Mattera Management and Yvonne Parks
Interior design: Katherine Lloyd
All photos used by permission of John Maisel and East-West Ministries. All rights reserved.

Cataloging-in-Publication Data is available.
ISBN: 978-1-7324353-1-5

Printed in the United States

DEDICATION FROM JOHN MAISEL

To Susie.

I am extremely humbled by the words in this book from men who have been the foundation of my life these past thirty years. Scripture is clear, "He who walks with wise men will be wise" (Proverbs 13:20, NASB), and I am profoundly grateful for their encouragement to me over these many decades. I am the subject of this book only because of the love and wise counsel I have received from these and many others during my life. I have run the race with better men than myself.

But the human cornerstone of my life has been my wife, Susie. Only the Lord and I know the depth of her love and sacrifices she has made over the years in God's calling on our lives together.

Yes, I am the public figure and she the private figure; both are high callings from our Lord. To me, she is the hero of the story. As I travel the world on an airplane, she travels it on her knees—both of us serving the Lord of all. But to me, she was making the greater sacrifice of many lonely weeks without contact.

I want to acknowledge publicly the tremendous sacrifices my wife, Susie, and my daughter, A'Dina, made when their soulmate as husband and father was gone. They prayed for me, not knowing if or when they would ever see me again.

I believe we focus too much of the time on the public part of our work for our Lord, but the angels of God are praising Him for all those working "behind the curtain," those who are fulfilling more important roles than we who have public platforms.

My wife is the hero of the faith for me. She had the harder part, and I want everyone to know she had the greater part from our Lord's perspective.

CONTENTS

Foreword by Dr. Jim Denison ix

Chapter 1: Meeting John Maisel 1

PART ONE: JOHN'S STORY

Chapter 2: A Man's Man 17

Chapter 3: The Road to Moscow 27

Chapter 4: Two Speeches at Moscow State University 41

Chapter 5: From Moscow to the World 57

PART TWO: JOHN'S MESSAGE

Chapter 6: The Necessity of Courage 89

Chapter 7: Take a Stand—No Matter What 101

Chapter 8: The Courage to Go Public 113

PART THREE: JOHN'S LEGACY

Chapter 9: A Mentor's Mentor 127

Chapter 10: Looking Toward the Future 139

Afterword by Kurt Nelson 151

Acknowledgments 155

About the Author 157

Notes 159

FOREWORD

It is unusual for a world-changing Christian to write the biography of another world-changing Christian. But that's the book you're now reading.

Our generation has seen no more transformative leaders than Mac Pier and John Maisel. They are truly a Peter and Paul for our day.

Peter was called to shepherd God's people (see Luke 22:32; John 21:15-17), working to strengthen their unity and encourage their witness (1 Peter 1:13-22). Continuing his calling today, Dr. Mac Pier is the most effective unifier of God's people I have ever seen.

I know of no one who combines intellectual brilliance and personal charisma as Mac does. Across six years of friendship and partnership together, I have seen the Spirit use Mac to unite and empower God's people in New York City, Dallas, and scores of cities around the globe.

If Mac Pier is a Peter for our day, John Maisel is a Paul. He is quite simply the most effective and anointed evangelist and missionary I have ever met.

I have known and admired John for thirty years. As you will read in Mac's compelling narrative, God took John from football fields in college and the NFL to the jungles of Vietnam, where he was wounded and received a Purple Heart. From military heroism to America's corporate boardrooms, to Moscow and evangelism behind the Iron Curtain, to founding a ministry that now circles the globe with the gospel, John has advanced the Kingdom like no one else in our generation.

Now you and I have John's story as only Mac could write it. Why did the Holy Spirit put this narrative in your hands? Two lessons from Paul's life and work help answer our question.

WE NEED MENTORS IN THE FAITH

Paul knew the importance of mentoring others. He invested himself in Timothy, Titus, Luke, and scores of others. The apostle even extended this remarkable invitation to his favorite congregation: "Whatever you have learned or received or heard from me, or seen in me—put it into practice. And the God of peace will be with you" (Philippians 4:9).

John Maisel would never offer such an invitation to us. He is too humble and too aware of his own shortcomings. So I'll make it instead.

For more than three decades, every time I have been with John, I have been inspired by him. Consider just one example.

John and I met for lunch recently in our North Dallas area. Ten minutes into our time together, he had learned the name of our server, asked her about her spiritual life, received permission to give her his gospel tract, and learned of ways we could pray for her.

If you travel with John, you'll watch him engage the flight attendants and nearby passengers in the same way.

He cannot stay at a hotel without sharing Christ with the employees he meets. He cannot preach a sermon or teach a Bible study without making certain that every person who hears him knows the gospel and has met Jesus personally.

I was senior pastor of First Baptist Church in Midland, Texas, when a church member first introduced me to John. A few minutes into our conversation, John asked me how I met Jesus. I could tell he was interested in more than the details of my story—he wanted to be sure that I knew his Lord.

Estimates suggest that 95 percent of all Christians have never led someone to Christ; less than 2 percent are involved in the ministry of evangelism.[1] We clearly need evangelistic examples to follow.

If John were writing these words, he would say: If I can share Christ with anyone, *you* can share Christ with anyone.

He's right.

WE NEED TO "EQUIP THE SAINTS" TODAY

Paul exhorted Christian leaders to "equip the saints for the work of ministry" (Ephesians 4:12, ESV). He knew that Christianity must multiply to reach the world.

Equipping disciples to make disciples is just as urgent today. In forty years of vocational ministry, the most common explanation I have heard from Christians who don't share their faith is that they don't know how.

This is unfortunately plausible. In a recent Barna survey, 51 percent of America's churchgoers said they had not heard the term "the Great Commission." Only 17 percent could identify its meaning accurately.[2]

We especially need to know how to share Jesus with adults. According to the American Culture & Faith Institute, 68 percent of those who accept Jesus as their Savior do so by the age of seventeen. Only 9 percent do so at forty years of age or older.[3]

John Maisel is as passionate about equipping Christians to share Jesus as he is about sharing the gospel himself. As a successful businessman, he understands the importance of leveraging resources to scale. As an athlete, he knows the value of effective coaching.

When you read his story, the Spirit will use it to help you make the Great Commission your commitment and lifestyle.

NOW IT'S OUR TURN

In his final letter, Paul exhorted his son in the faith: "The things you have heard me say in the presence of many witnesses entrust to reliable people who will also be qualified to teach others" (2 Timothy 2:2).

It's been rightly noted that Christianity is always one generation from extinction. What God has done through Mac Pier and John Maisel, He wants to do through us. That's why you are holding John's biography now.

One of John's favorite aphorisms is, "Don't drop the flag." His story, and the message he has given his life to share, are now in your hands.

—Dr. Jim Denison

Chief Executive Officer, Denison Forum

JOHN MAISEL'S PERSONAL MISSION STATEMENT

I exist to point people to Jesus.

If they are outside of Jesus Christ, I point them to the cross of Christ and the bodily resurrection of Jesus Christ. His resurrection conquered death for all who receive Him as their personal Lord and Savior. If they have received Jesus Christ as their Lord and Savior, I point them to the grace of God and Jesus' indwelling presence. Whomever I meet, whenever I meet them, and however I meet them, I exist to point people to the love of Christ and the power and presence of His indwelling life.

—John Maisel
1991

CHAPTER 1

MEETING JOHN MAISEL

I did not meet John Maisel until after his seventieth birthday. What struck me initially about John is that you don't really meet him; you *encounter* him. John is a tornado of passion and energy all rolled into one person.

I've known him for more than eight years, and I've found that passion and energy to be consistent in his life, even though now, at age seventy-eight, he is living with an incurable fibrosis of the lungs. Nothing—not even a terminal illness—stops John from pursuing his mission to further the Kingdom of God. He is totally sold out—all in—to the cause of Christ. In fact, as I and the hundreds of other people who know John can attest, he is the closest we've ever seen to someone being like the apostle Paul. In every moment, John lives out Paul's testimony from Philippians 3:12-14:

> Not that I have already obtained all this, or have already arrived at my goal, but I press on to take

hold of that for which Christ Jesus took hold of me. Brothers and sisters, I do not consider myself yet to have taken hold of it. But one thing I do: Forgetting what is behind and straining toward what is ahead, I press on toward the goal to win the prize for which God has called me heavenward in Christ Jesus.

As John's time on this earth draws to a close, many of my colleagues and I have realized that his story needs to be told. We need to carry on the eternal work and to inspire future generations to learn at the feet of a once-in-a-generation kind of leader. The world needs a thousand leaders like John to take on the enormous challenges facing the church and society. You can't encounter John and not be encouraged, challenged, and motivated to keep pressing on in our mission. That has certainly been true of my experience with him.

To understand my journey with John, let me provide the historical backdrop to our initial meeting. I began traveling monthly to Dallas in 2011 to meet with Jim Runyan, the board chairman of an organization I was leading called The New York City Leadership Center, now Movement.org. We also met with Jeff Warren, pastor of Park Cities Baptist Church, to birth Movement Day DFW (Dallas-Fort Worth), patterned after Movement Day in New York City.[1]

Early in one of those first trips to Dallas I met John. We bumped into each other at the East-West offices in Plano. East-West's offices are located at The Hope Center, which houses forty mission agencies. I was visiting June Hunt, founder of The Hope Center. She had been an early partner with Movement Day, and we were planning for a future presentation.

John was full of energy. I could tell from our initial interaction that he really cared about the work that East-West was about. He gave me a copy of *Radical Trust,* a book he wrote that emphasizes two main messages from God to His followers: *I love you* and *Trust Me.* He encouraged me to read it. I took in his enthusiasm, looked again at the book's title, and thought *radical* was a good way to summarize John.

I knew of John through his work as the founder of East-West Ministries, a mission organization that he began in 1993 to mobilize Christian leaders to share the gospel in the hardest places by planting house churches. More formally, "The vision of East-West is to glorify God by multiplying followers of Jesus in the spiritually darkest areas of the world." Their official mission statement is that they exist "to mobilize the Body of Christ to evangelize the lost and equip local believers to multiply disciples and healthy churches among unreached peoples and/or in restricted access communities."[2]

This organization's work fit perfectly with what Movement.org was doing, and I was thrilled to have them join our ranks in helping to plan the Movement Day DFW event. John had attended one of the early Movement Day events in New York City. Every year fifty leaders from the Dallas area attended the event. John contacted me after Movement Day in New York City in 2012, because he wanted to propose a partnership between Movement Day and Explore God. Explore God, a ministry separate from East-West, was a vehicle to allow churches to creatively work together in cities to share the gospel.

It seemed appropriate that my friendship with John was rooted in his desire to accelerate the work of the gospel through Explore God just as he was doing with East-West. And I knew that Movement Day could be an important platform to introduce Explore God to dozens of cities in the United States. The partnership was exciting—and successful.

Thanks to John's tireless efforts, Explore God and Movement Day introduced Explore God to a variety of church networks in Dallas. One conversation was with Bob Dean, the executive director of the Dallas Baptist Association (DBA). There are more than seven hundred churches involved with the DBA. By 2016, four hundred churches in Dallas were ready to host a fall campaign using Explore God's content and resources. And in Austin the Explore God campaign involved another four hundred churches and stimulated thousands of spiritual conversations. The model has been picked up by dozens of cities around the world. Much of this success was all because John never gave up his vision to reach as many people as possible with the gospel.

JOHN AND EXPLORE GOD

In 2006 John was speaking at Hill Country Bible Church in Austin, Texas, when he met Dan Smith, a CEO with Creditcard.com. They were mutual friends of Hill Country's pastor, Tim Hawks. At the service, John spoke about 113 church plants in many of the most difficult mission fields in the world that East-West had birthed at the cost of one thousand dollars per church plant. Dan and his wife were so impressed by what East-West was doing, they determined to help as they could.

"My company had been experiencing success," Dan said. "We walked up to John after the service and handed him a check for $113,000 for the next 113 church plants."

That initial encounter flourished into a friendship around a common passion for the gospel. By the next year Dan asked John to partner with him to start an organization that would work to make the gospel accessible and friendly, especially to the next generation. John was in the process of stepping down from his CEO role of East-West, so he agreed. John, Dan, and a team they assembled spent six to eight hours each meeting in white-board sessions formulating that organization, which eventually became Explore God.[3]

But John's influence wasn't limited to his work with Explore God. He affected Dan, who calls John his spiritual father. "He has changed my life forever," Dan said, offering this example.

Several years ago John invited Dan to attend an East-West banquet. The guest speaker was President George W. Bush. On the evening of the banquet, John escorted Dan toward the front of the room, indicating he had made arrangements for Dan and his group. When John stopped at the head table, Dan was stunned. A seat for him was waiting—and it was next to the forty-third president of the United States. "Without any fanfare John wanted me to have a seat of honor," said Dan. "I believe he wanted me to experience President Bush as just an ordinary person, a follower of Jesus."

A MAN OF UNDYING PASSION

John is unapologetically passionate about the unity of the church and introducing people to the gospel. Anyone who has spent any time with him will remember those encounters in restaurants. It does not matter who the server is, John will always appropriately engage. He will ask a question to find out something about the person. That response will naturally segue into a spiritual question. And if he finds the server receptive to their conversation, he will leave behind one of the booklets he's authored, *Is Jesus God?* or *The Gift of God* or *Can I Really Know for Sure?* He even has them ready in different languages to make sure the language doesn't become a barrier to the person hearing about Christ.

John is present to everyone he meets. He is genuinely interested in the other person. He is fearless in his presentation of the gospel. His faith is infectious.

That extends to his family. For many leaders, all too often we hear stories that they "won the world but lost their family." This hasn't been the case for John, according to his only child, A'Dina Smith (no relation to Explore God's Dan Smith), who described her relationship with her dad as being extremely close. "Though my dad began to travel extensively in my high school years when East-West started, he was very present when he was home," she said. "My dad would take me on a date every Saturday when he was home. He is the same way with my children today. As a former college football player, he loves to watch my son play football."

John also instilled several lessons in her life. "He said the number-one thing is to always be graceful and to not give up on other people. He said that everyone is somebody."

She saw that he practiced what he preached. While she was growing up, they encountered a homeless person. "My dad's number-one concern is that any homeless person would know how much Jesus cared for them," she said. One time when he had taken a homeless person for a meal, John was struck by how blue the man's eyes were. John got up to pay for the meal and returned to find the homeless person gone. "He wondered if he had entertained an angel unaware," A'Dina said.

A'Dina, married to her high school sweetheart and the mother of two children, one in college and one in high school, thinks a lot about her dad's legacy. "My dad's primary message is about the grace of God in the Person of Jesus," she said. "He wants everyone to experience the grace of God in Jesus and to be gracious toward one another."

His greatest reward? A'Dina said, "I know that my dad will hear, 'good and faithful servant' from Jesus at the end of his life. I want that to be said of me and of my family as well."

THE THEMES OF JOHN MAISEL'S LIFE

As we look back over John's life, we can break it down in eight themes, which we'll look at more closely throughout the book. But I'd like us to consider these themes, not only as a tribute to who John is but also to encourage and motivate us in our lives and ministry as well.

1. Be Passionate by Being "All In" All the Time

John was a successful athlete, having played quarterback in high school as well as at Oklahoma State University. He also received an offer to play professional football for the Houston Oilers.

After college John entered the Marines as a lieutenant in the Vietnam War. He received the Purple Heart after being injured and a Bronze Star for valor. For many, those things would be enough to give a person their identity—but not for John. John's identity is in Christ, but he brings his passion for athletics, military, and business into his life with God. He teaches us that we should be "all in" whatever our position in life is.

2. Life Is Temporary, So We Must Be Urgent in Our Work

While in Vietnam, John learned powerful spiritual lessons about the temporary nature of life. He was surrounded by death daily. He saw many of his friends enter eternity in their twenties. We don't have time to wait, even when we aren't involved in a physical war—because there's a spiritual war going on. John recognized that and used every moment to bring people to the winning side of the "war."

3. People in the Darkest Parts of the World Need to Hear the Good News

Having served in Vietnam, John saw the effects that closed societies, such as Vietnam, Russia, and Cuba, have on their people. John's response was to become part of a team that worked underground, behind the Iron Curtain in the 1980s until the Berlin Wall came down in 1989. This team of brothers and sisters was called BEE (Biblical Education Extension), and out of this ministry came the vision for East-West, after the fall of the Iron Curtain. Living through the horrors of war uniquely prepared John for the spiritual battlefields of the least-reached places on the planet. His ministry "grit" to go where others don't offers us a glimpse of what God is calling us to as well.

4. Work with Abandon

One of my favorite "Maiselisms" is "Don't drop the flag." In other words, never give up. Stay fully committed to the very end. He often retells the story from Joe Gibbs, former coach of the Washington Redskins, about how a football game is played: "For the first three quarters of the game, you work hard to score and to stay ahead of your opponent. In the final quarter and especially in the final two minutes of the game, you need to play with abandonment to accomplish victory."

5. Live with the Urgency of Immediacy

John will bring up in nearly every conversation that the only two days that matter are "*today* and *that day*." John lives with the urgency of immediacy because of the reality of eternity. *This day* is today and *that day* is the day when everyone stands before God in judgment. John believes that if we have those two days squarely in our sights, we will make informed choices and will always help point other people to the Person of Jesus as Savior and Lord.

6. We Can't Afford to Be Silent

John calls it "the epidemic of silence" and is gravely concerned by the growing number of young people who are leaving the church. He believes that a tiny fraction of the followers of Jesus are actually sharing their faith in any kind of consistent way. He believes that people have been shamed into being silent about their faith. John's antidote to this silence is for believers to take the courageous posture of looking for every opportunity to build a bridge to share the gospel with those we encounter. The believer is to be on mission twenty-four hours a day, seven days a week, as they interact with other people. He believes we always have opportunity all around us to point others to Christ.

7. One Dedicated Person Can Change the World

John believes it takes just one person who says yes to God, who dives in headfirst with passion and commitment, to see God work in the world. John is living proof. He never allows the idea that he can't do something for God just because it will take too many people or too much money or more than one of anything. He steps in and shows up and then waits for God to do the rest. When he founded East-West, he believed that same idea. One person, one church, one of anything can be the spark to ignite the Holy Spirit's flame. Today, East-West is a remarkable global movement that is multiplying churches around the world in the hardest places. East-West has convened thousands of business leaders for the past twenty-five years to cast vision for impacting the gospel around the world.

8. Our Lives Are Powerful Influencers

John's most significant contribution at this season of his life is his regular interaction with Christian business leaders. He leads three to four Bible studies with men in Dallas every week when he's not traveling. He does this to invest in the spiritual well-being of marketplace men living extraordinarily demanding lives. John is committed to keeping them grounded in their faith and to challenging them to be "all in." He believes it is important for all of us to assess where we have influence over others—at home, in the neighborhood, on campus, and at the workplace. We need to seize those opportunities to influence those around us.

BEING "ALL IN"

As we've mentioned earlier, you can talk with anyone who has spent time with John and they'll tell you the same thing—he's the closest thing they've experienced to meeting the apostle Paul.

I've found the same to be true in my experiences with him. As we work our way through this book, examining John's life and what makes it so amazing, I will weave in analogies between John's life and that of Paul's.

In his biography of Paul by the same name, N. T. Wright answered the question, "What made Paul, Paul?" In the story of Paul's conversion in Acts 9, Wright said that "Saul (later Paul) had an explosion of truth in his mind and in his heart."[4] That explosion would forever change Paul and put him on his trajectory to plant churches among the Gentile cities of Asia and Europe. That trajectory also led him to write thirteen of the twenty-seven books of the New Testament and 28 percent of its content.

In the story of Acts 9, Paul encountered Christ, who asked him this question: "Saul, Saul, why do you persecute me?" (verse 4). I found this to be the most interesting question in the New Testament. Jesus didn't ask, "Saul, Saul, why are you persecuting the church?" But rather, "Why are you persecuting me?"

Because of Jesus' intimacy with the church, to persecute the church was to persecute Jesus. Jesus was out of patience with Paul's destruction of His church and confronted Him with a yes-or-no encounter on the road to Damascus. Prior to his conversion Paul had caused the church to suffer as the result of his persecution. Though John isn't similar to Paul in this regard, he does understand and has been able to identify with the suffering church in the persecuted parts of the world. He has made many trips where his family had no contact with him for weeks.

Paul would forever be changed by this Jesus who knew him by name. Paul would forever be changed by this Jesus who identified so intimately with His church. Paul would forever be changed in that same Acts 9 passage by a visitor named Ananias.

Jesus called Ananias to visit Paul on Straight Street in Damascus (verse 11). Ananias had heard about Paul and his dastardly reputation, so understandably, he was nervous about encountering the most violent persecutor of the church in the first century. But Jesus told him, "Go! This man is my chosen instrument to proclaim my name to the

Gentiles and their kings and to the people of Israel. I will show him how much he must suffer for my name" (verses 15-16). We see from Jesus' statement that from the early days of Paul's conversion, Paul knew he had a date with Rome to preach the gospel. The king of the Gentiles was Caesar and he lived in Rome. Rome was at that time the most powerful city in human history.

Ananias traveled to the house in Damascus on Straight Street as instructed. Upon seeing Paul blind and helpless, he placed his hand on Paul's shoulder. Ananias then uttered the two most tender words of the New Testament, "Brother Saul."

The destroyer of the church and the one imprisoning followers of the Way was now part of the family. Paul would never forget that moment. From then on, he began and ended every one of his letters with a reference to the grace of God.

This theme of grace is woven deeply into John Maisel's life as well. It comes from six decades of passionately following Jesus and six decades of being immersed in the words of Paul, along with all of Scripture.

Paul wrote his letter to the Philippians near the end of his life in AD 61 or AD 62. It was in Philippi that Paul planted the first European church. It was the church in Philippi where the early members brought three very different classes of people together—a businesswoman named Lydia, a slave girl, and a jailer. From Philippi, the gospel spread across Europe to Athens, Corinth, Thessalonica, and eventually to Rome. Rome was the political capital of the world, just as Jerusalem was the religious capital of the world.

The church in Philippi represented a new frontier, just as John's work in East-West has represented a new frontier in the Muslim, Hindu, and communist worlds. As Paul wrote from his prison cell near the end of his life, he stated that he pressed on to take hold of the prize that he had in Christ Jesus (Philippians 3:14). He was "all in" even to the end of his life. John has patterned his life after this theme.

I invite you to join the journey with us in reading this biography of John Maisel. Use this simple reflection to ask yourself if you are "all in" on the purposes that God has for you. John was. I pray you will do the same.

PART ONE

JOHN'S STORY

CHAPTER 2

A MAN'S MAN

John Maisel was born in Temple, Texas, in 1940, one year after the start of World War II. He had one sister, Pat, who was five years older. For the first five years of John's life, his parents ran an orphanage in Fort Worth, but they later moved the family to Texarkana, where both his parents taught school and his father coached football.

While his parents ran the orphanage, John spent time with an African-American couple who cared for him and his sister. Little did he know at the time that his experience in that cross-cultural and ethnic relationship would lay an important foundation for his future global mission, as "being raised by an African-American couple caused me to develop a love for those from African-American backgrounds," he said years later.

John grew up attending a local Methodist church with his family. Although the family didn't study the Bible at home, John's father did pray with him most evenings.

By the time John started high school at Texarkana High, he was already excelling as an athlete and played quarterback for his team. He also had a football scholarship to play at Oklahoma State University, and by his senior year, he was captain and voted most valuable player. Though he loved sports, at the time he didn't realize how God would use that love to shape His mission for John's life. John's athleticism would give him confidence that would serve him in each season—military, marketplace, and global mission.

While he was in high school, something else exceptional began to take place in John's life. He began to sense a thirst for spiritual things, so he started reading the Bible at night. During his senior year in 1958, he attended a revival meeting where he made a faith commitment. "My life radically changed," he admitted.

When he told his mother about his newfound faith, she did not know what to think of it and told him he was already a Christian and did not need to make, what she called, such "a radical change." But that didn't stop John from pursuing his new life in Christ.

After he graduated in 1958, he attended Oklahoma State University on a full athletic scholarship. While there, he saw God's hand on him, continuing to help him grow in his faith, as he discovered his freshman coach was a Navigator alumnus. The Navigators were a ministry birthed after World War II, in which their core emphasis was on Bible study and memorization.

His coach took John under his wing and mentored him in his new faith. As he continued in his studies and sports, he felt led to help plant a chapter of the Fellowship of Christian Athletes (FCA) on campus. He became very active in sharing his faith on campus and told his testimony as often as he could in sororities and fraternities. But he admits that being new in the faith, he had a lot of grounding he still needed.

During those years he also met a young woman, Susie, who caught his eye on campus at Oklahoma State University. Before they graduated, Susie became his wife.

Something else happened before he graduated. The Houston Oilers drafted him. He left the university to become a professional football player. When he did not make the team as a player, he returned to OSU to coach the freshman football team and to finish college, graduating in 1963 with a degree in business and a minor in philosophy.

During his time at school, since every male student was supposed to have two years of military service, John joined the Reserved Officer Training Corp (ROTC) of the Marines. Then after he graduated, to fulfill his ROTC agreement at Oklahoma State University, John joined the Marines full time to serve for three years, entering as a second lieutenant. As with his other choices, this decision would also change his life. But more so even, this decision would forever change his faith and his mission.

VIETNAM AND THE FORMATION OF JOHN MAISEL'S FAITH

When John joined the Marines, the Vietnam War was already in full swing, having started in 1955, so he knew the chances of being deployed to a war zone were high. Sure enough, the following year, in 1964, he left his new bride, Susie, stateside and headed with his platoon to the other side of the world to engage in a conflict that many in the United States didn't approve of or understand.

The United States and Russia had been allies in World War II to defeat Hitler, but it was an uneasy marriage. With Soviet expansion during the 1950s and 1960s across Europe and Asia, President John F. Kennedy announced in his January 1961 inauguration speech, "We will pay any price, we will bear any burden, meet any hardship, support any friend, oppose any foe to assure the survival and success of liberty."[1]

The Vietnam War represented the ideological collision course between America's vision of democracy and the Soviet Union's vision for a world dominated by communism. For months John found himself in the middle of the conflict, before he was shot and wounded, giving him an honorable discharge.

During that time, John's faith went from his head to his heart. Being in the crucible of war caused John to come to grips with several life-and-death realities, and the message of God's sovereignty and love for him became a living reality.

He recounted the experience of capturing a Vietcong man who was part of a team trying to kill John's unit. When they first captured the man, John was furious and threw the man to the ground. But the Spirit of God convicted him, speaking Jesus' words to him from Matthew 5:44, "Love your enemies," and from Proverbs 25:21, "If your enemy is hungry, give him food to eat." John calmed down and did something that surprised everyone. As his fellow marines objected, John extended his canteen to the trembling Vietcong in order to give him something to drink. Then he reached down and picked the man up off the ground. John knew, as a follower of Jesus, he needed to live a different kind of way, even toward enemy combatants.

For some of his tour, he was part of a team assigned to locate the Vietcong. They scouted areas, usually from a submarine or helicopter. When he was in the submarine, he spent hours cooped up at times without much to do, so he used most of that time lying on his bunk and studying the life of David. During those lonely, quiet hours, God made the life of David come alive to him. Through his extended reflection, John considered David's life as a soldier and how he expressed his love for God in that context. That seemed to open a love affair with the Scriptures John had begun in high school, which continued to grow during his deployment.

He also engaged the soldiers in spiritual conversations and shared the gospel whenever he could. He admits there were times when soldiers would tell him, "Lieutenant, no, I'm not really interested."

But as he began to see these same men getting hit in battle, he realized he couldn't hold back. Often he held fellow soldiers as they died in his arms. Being that close to young men who breathed their last breath greatly affected him.

Almost every person John saw hit before they died had a scared look on their faces. "Almost to the person," he said, "they would cry out, 'Oh, God, don't let me die. Oh, God, help me.'"

Watching those soldiers at that critical stage of breathing their last breath made John realize how urgent it was for him to get "the message of the redeeming love of Jesus Christ to as many people as possible."

One day John and his team were getting ready to go on an operation. The night before they were on an aircraft carrier and were going into the battlefield by choppers. That night, John stood on guard duty with a young marine named Jim Husbeth. It was pitch black on the ship, so they could barely see anything in front of them. Into that darkness, John began talking to the man about knowing Jesus. After he shared the gospel with him and had a great conversation, John took his leave.

"Hey, it's getting late," he said. "I've got an operation tomorrow. I've got to turn in."

The next day John and his men boarded the choppers, headed inland, and landed on a hill. They discovered that the Vietcong had been there and booby-trapped it, burying landmines all over.

"Men, we need to clear the hill of whatever booby traps, mines that might be here," John told his men.

They formed a skirmish line and walked very slowly and carefully with their bayonets, trying to see anything unusual. For some reason that John can't explain, he got out in front of the skirmish line and walked. He was unaware he had stepped over a booby trap, but after he was a few steps ahead of his men, a marine behind him stepped directly on an 81-mm mortar booby trap. The explosion came immediately, blowing the marine up in the air. Just as the explosion happened, the Vietcong charged in an ambush.

"Don't let me die!" the wounded marine shouted. "Somebody help me!"

John was the closest to him, so he crawled over and

while the other soldiers handled the ambush, John protected the marine by lying on top of him. He started to pray over the marine, not sure if the man would survive or not.

"Lieutenant," the man shouted. "I'm the one you talked to about Jesus last night."

The medic chopper finally arrived and carried the wounded marine away. But John didn't know what had happened to the man. He just knew he had done whatever he could to help prepare the marine for this life or his eternal one.

John continued his work in Vietnam, fighting the physical and the spiritual enemy. But he didn't get out unscathed. In 1965, after being in Vietnam for less than a year, he was wounded three days before he was set to leave the warfront.

DISCOVERING THE REALITY AND COMFORT OF PSALM 23

For John Maisel, ending up in Vietnam was not accidental. God used all the historical forces of the twentieth century to lead him to that experience. Though his time in Vietnam lasted only several months, it shaped the trajectory of the next fifty years. He saw the captivity of people in communism and felt the urgency to get the gospel to as many people as possible, as urgently as possible, and as simply as possible.

Being a marine in Vietnam was living in the shadow of the valley of death. There were tens of thousands of twenty-somethings who would never return home. The David whom John encountered on the submarine was the same David who pointed to a Great Shepherd who was involved in every detail of John's life, as *he* walked through the valley of the shadow of death.

The beauty of that urgency was that he got to see some of the fruit of his work.

Eight or nine years later, now back in the States, John was at an aerobics center getting a massage. The massage therapist who was working on him commented on the scar on John's leg.

"I got shot in Vietnam," he told the man.

"I know a guy who was in Vietnam," the massage therapist said. "He had both his legs blown off."

"Really? What branch was he in?"

"Marines."

John's interest was piqued. "When was he there?"

"The mid-1960s."

"What was his name?" John asked.

"Jim Husbeth."

John lifted himself off the table in shock and said, "Let me tell you the story of Jim Husbeth." And after some prompting, the massage therapist gave Jim's phone number to John.

John called the number. When Jim answered, John said, "I don't know if I've got the right Jim Husbeth, but let me tell you this story." He shared the story of that fateful day in Vietnam, as the man silently listened. When he got to the point where John crawled over him and was praying for him, he couldn't remember what he was praying.

Was it the Lord's Prayer? Was I quoting a verse or something? he wondered. So he said, "After I crawled over, I started praying the Lord's Prayer."

"No, sir." Jim Husbeth finally interrupted John's story. "It was the Twenty-third Psalm." Then he further surprised John by telling him he wanted to fly to Texas to see him.

John agreed, but told him, "I want to send you a little booklet of a lecture called *Is Jesus God?* I want you to read it and I want to discuss it with you."

"Yes, sir, I will do that."

Several days later Jim showed up in his wheelchair. They had an incredible reunion, during which they discussed their time together in Vietnam. Finally, John began to talk again about spiritual things.

"Let me make clear what the gospel really means," he told Jim. Then he proceeded to walk Jim through the gospel and asked him if he understood it. When Jim nodded, John said, "Would you like to pray the prayer of receiving Christ and trusting Christ personally?"

Jim smiled. "I prayed it after I read the book, sir."

God is the Great Guide who led John into paths of righteousness for His name's sake. That pathway led him into war zones and booby traps. It led him to plead with young men going into battle that Jesus was a Savior offering them eternal life whether they returned home or not.

In a way, he was living Psalm 23 on the battlefield. He embraced David's words:

The LORD is my shepherd, I lack nothing.
He makes me lie down in green pastures,
he leads me beside quiet waters,
he refreshes my soul.
He guides me along the right paths for his name's sake.
Even though I walk through the darkest valley,
I will fear no evil, for you are with me;

your rod and your staff, they comfort me.
You prepare a table before me in the presence of my
enemies.
You anoint my head with oil; my cup overflows.
Surely your goodness and love will follow me all the
days of my life,
and I will dwell in the house of the LORD forever.

In that psalm, David promised that the Lord is our shepherd and that we shall not want. But for John to live and share that truth in the context of the war in Vietnam is remarkable. Of course there is want: people are dying, countries are being torn up, and entire communities are being decimated. How could David say that? How could John say it—and believe it?

John could say it because he embraced God's greatest gift to us—the Lord's presence. God's presence is so great that even in the midst of danger and death, John could say, "I shall not want." In fact, the presence of God is so great that compared to any other need, John could live and believe it with confidence that "I shall not want." And he wanted his soldiers to know that truth as well. He spent his time in battle showing the power of God's presence.

Just as David could reflect on his life at the end of his life in Psalm 23 as shepherd, warrior, refugee, musician, and king, John reflects on the end of his life anticipating his union with the great Lover of his soul. John's mission has always been to remember that there are only two days: today and that day. Times are urgent, and John wants us to understand that it is paramount that we introduce people to the Great Shepherd.

CHAPTER 3

THE ROAD TO MOSCOW

By 1965, John was winding down his thirteen-month deployment in Vietnam. As men neared the end of their service in Vietnam, normally they would not be sent out on a combat mission for fear of injury or fatality. John was different. He volunteered to go on missions knowing that if he were killed, he had eternal security in his relationship with Jesus.

"I was more concerned that a fellow soldier would be shot and killed, unprepared to meet his Maker," John said. He was making those calculations as a twenty-five-year-old.

In his last mission John was shot and wounded in the leg. He needed to be hospitalized, so the Marines flew him out of Vietnam. For the better part of a year, he recovered in a military hospital in the Philippines, and then was flown back to the United States for another operation. His healing took a year. After he was released from the hospital, he was honorably discharged from the Marines. He received a Purple Heart medal for being wounded and for his bravery in battle and a Bronze Star for valor.

Now with the war behind him and his future bright ahead of him, John chose a business path for his career. He started working in the insurance business and later moved into the investment arena of real estate. He got involved with real estate in 1966 with another businessman, Richard Ford. As the business became more successful, they ended up selling the company. And by 1976, John's workplace emphasis shifted from real estate to energy. With longtime friend Pat Booth, he founded the Shekinah Oil and Gas Company and served as its president.

During that time he began to wrestle with where he felt God calling him. He started to pray, asking God to lead him in whether he should attend seminary and go into ministry, or continue in business and become a self-supporting missionary in the marketplace. He felt God tell him to remain in the marketplace.

Although a successful businessman, John was still an evangelist at heart and continued sharing the gospel wherever he went and with whomever he encountered. He saw firsthand how working in the marketplace was a high and holy calling for every marketplace Christian.

What was perhaps most surprising about his work was that he sought out Vietnamese refugees, for whom he had developed an affection. Despite the horrors of the Vietnam War, John saw past the political landscape and ideology and looked at the people as God saw them—deeply loved and wondrously created in the image of God. That meant John had a responsibility to share God's love with them as well.

He began to employ Vietnamese boat people—eighty to ninety worked for his business—and invited them to Bible studies he led for his employees. As Vietnamese refugees came to faith in Jesus, John set up a baptismal tank in the warehouse.

His company was doing well, and he felt committed to the work he was involved with. Then in 1986, the world began to shift in dramatic ways.

SETTING THE STAGE TOWARD MOSCOW

In 1985, while John was still acting as president for Shekinah Oil and Gas Company, on the other side of the world, Mikhail Gorbachev had come to power in the Soviet Union. Under one of the largest governments operating from a communist political ideology, the nation was falling apart and in desperate need of economic reforms. Gorbachev's leadership was forward thinking and reform minded. He recognized that communism was failing in his country, with the general consensus being discontentment with the political landscape. He wanted to introduce a broad policy of economic restructuring, which he called *perestroika*. According to Thoughtco. com writer Tarkan Rosenberg, Gorbachev "needed to get the people on his side to put pressure on the bureaucrats, so he introduced two new policies: *glasnost* (meaning openness) and *demokratizatsiyz* (democratization). These policies were intended to encourage ordinary Russian citizens to openly voice their concern and unhappiness with the regime."[1]

Back in the United States, President Ronald Reagan had emerged as the greatest global champion for democracy in his generation. Reagan had been a longtime opponent of communism dating back to his acting career in California in the 1940s and 1950s. He brought that opposition with him into the White House. Yet he also knew the art of diplomacy and worked to forge a friendship with Mikhail Gorbachev— one that would ultimately contribute to dismantling the Soviet Union as the world knew it in 1989.

As the political landscape appeared to be changing for the Soviet Union, a strong spiritual wind was shifting as well, something John kept his eyes on. Pope John Paul II spoke out against communism, urging the people toward faith in Christ. Evangelist Billy Graham rose up as well and preached in communist East Germany, Czechoslovakia, and Romania between 1982 and 1985. In Romania, Graham drew a crowd of one hundred and fifty thousand who responded so enthusiastically that the country's dictator, Nicolae Ceausescu, feared an uprising and canceled a meeting with Graham.

The stage was being set through the convergence of political, economic, and spiritual forces for the gospel to move forcefully into the heart of the communist capital of the world. And in 1986, Congressman Jack Kemp convened a meeting of religious leaders and Christian businessmen, including John, to discuss the current state of the Soviet Union and how to make inroads there for the gospel.

Kemp shared a lot in common with John. They both were men of faith. Also a football player, the congressman had been an NFL quarterback with the Buffalo Bills. And they had both been in the military, with Jack Kemp serving in the army from 1958 to 1962. During that time, he saw firsthand the brutality of communism from both the Korean War and the Vietnam War.

During the meeting, the group agreed that they wanted to move forward by putting together several agencies to form a consortium to take the gospel behind the Iron Curtain. It seemed the right time to "strike," so to speak. And John was going to be a big part of it.

THE APOSTLE PAUL'S TRIP TO ROME COMPARED TO JOHN'S TRIP TO MOSCOW

John was on a trajectory to get to Moscow. He had been immersed in the battle against communism in Vietnam. The Vietnam War was a proxy war between the United States and the communism of Russia and China. All of John's life experiences and spiritual experiences were preparing him for this encounter. Just as Paul's experiences prepared him for his.

Before the apostle Paul's miraculous conversion, he had been focused almost exclusively on what theologian and author N. T. Wright described as twin themes: Torah and Temple.[2] The Torah represented the sacred Jewish Scriptures. Paul was fascinated by Scripture's account in Numbers 25 of Phineas, a Levitical priest, who was very zealous. Phineas stopped the Lord's judgment of sending a plague against the Israelites by spearing to death an Israelite man and Moabite woman caught in sexual immorality. Because of Phineas's zeal, God ascribed to Phineas as the one who made the Lord turn away His anger against the Israelites. Paul's imagination was captured by Phineas's zeal.

It was Paul's misplaced zeal toward the early church that resulted in the imprisonment and execution of early Christians. But on that road to Damascus (see Acts 9), Jesus confronted Paul with an explosion of truth by revealing that Jesus was the fulfillment of both the Torah and the Temple. Paul realized as he reread the Scriptures that the Law of Moses, the prophecies of Elijah, and the psalms of David pointed toward a coming Jewish Messiah—Jesus.

Just as Moses instituted the Passover, Paul saw that Jesus became the ultimate Passover Lamb. Jesus was both Great High Priest and Sacrificial Lamb. Jesus was the very temple of God, God become man. This truth in Paul's mind and heart recategorized everything he thought he understood about the purposes of God in the world.

Why is this important? Because it changed the mission of Paul. No longer was he interested in persecuting the church; he was called to grow it. Jesus had a clear mission for Paul, and His directive came through Ananias who told Paul that he would be a witness to the Gentiles and to their kings.

Who was the king of the Gentiles? Caesar.

Where was Caesar? Rome.

Paul discerned early in his spiritual journey that he had a date with Rome. He would interpret the rest of his life circumstances through the vision to get there.

At that point Rome was the most influential city in human history. It was not coincidental that Christianity flourished during this period. One of the great themes of human and biblical history is that God is drawing people to the great cities of the world for His redemptive purposes. Jesus died in Jerusalem—the religious capital of the world—and Paul died in Rome—the political capital of the world. God has used the influence of cities to advance spiritual purposes. The Bible culminates in Revelation in the New Jerusalem, where people from every tribe and tongue are gathered to worship. The Roman Empire stretched from northwestern Europe to the Near East and encompassed all the lands surrounding the Mediterranean.

What better way to grow God's church than by using the Roman Empire? At the time of Jesus' ascension, the Christian movement was at about twenty-five thousand followers. By the year AD 312, when Constantine, the Roman emperor, declared himself to be a Christian, that number was twenty million. Christianity grew eight hundred times in three hundred years through the cities of the Roman Empire.[3] That was God's plan for the church. He would use the Roman Empire as His vehicle to grow His church. And part of that plan was to use Paul, the apostle to the Gentiles, to initiate that movement.

It is important that we see the analogy between the global significance of Rome in the first century and the global significance of Moscow in the twentieth century. Rome's empire spanned five hundred years. The communistic empire did not last nearly as long, but its reach was far greater geographically than that of Rome.

Through both of those empires, God was preparing the way for people to hear the gospel. The Roman Empire prepared people to be connected to the gospel through the

Roman roads. These roads allowed the gospel to travel faster than any other religious philosophy in history.

The Communist Empire of Russia created a spiritual void in people's lives through its atheism. For many this prepared a receptivity to the gospel that John and his team would communicate into.

In Acts 23:11, we read God's mission to Paul: "The following night the Lord stood near Paul and said, 'Take courage! As you have testified about me in Jerusalem, so you must also testify in Rome.'" Just as God prepared Paul, the first-century Jew, to preach the gospel in Rome, God also prepared John Maisel, a Vietnam veteran and businessman, to preach the gospel in Moscow. The pattern of God from the beginning of time has been to connect His providence to His purpose.

In His providence God prepared Paul as a multilingual Jew who was also a Roman citizen from Tarsus to take the gospel to the Gentiles throughout Asia and Europe. Paul was uniquely qualified in his giftings to be able to craft an apology (explanation) for the gospel in any context—whether it be to challenge the philosophies of the Athenians or to question the hedonism of the Corinthians.

In His providence God also uniquely prepared John to become a missionary to the communist world and beyond. His battlefield experience in Vietnam, his skills as an athlete to act with great agility, his strong business sense, and his deep love and knowledge of Scripture prepared him for his world-changing assignment.

God births movements from strategic cities and has been doing this for thousands of years. For instance, David captured Jerusalem three thousand years ago (see 2 Samuel 5) and still today it remains the religious capital of the world. Jesus' death just outside Jerusalem was not accidental. He said multiple times in the Gospels that He had to go to Jerusalem and die there. From Jerusalem God initiated the birth of the Christian movement at Pentecost (see Acts 2).

And God used Jerusalem to get Paul to Rome, another strategic city where God's plans would be carried out. During one of Paul's journeys, he traveled to Jerusalem, as recorded in Acts 21. While he was presenting himself in the Temple, some people discovered who he was in relation to the new-found Christ-followers. They mobbed him with the intent to execute him. He was arrested and found himself in prison. In that circumstance Paul might have been tempted to think it was game over.

Two remarkable things happened. During the night while Paul was in prison, Jesus came and spoke to him. He told Paul, "Take courage! As you have testified about me in Jerusalem, so you must also testify in Rome." In Paul's darkest hour in prison, he needed the reminder that Jesus was providentially guiding his life. But how would Paul get to Rome when he was sitting in a dark cell in Jerusalem?

He would appeal to Caesar—the second remarkable piece of the puzzle. He could have been released from prison on the grounds that he was a Roman citizen. But Paul chose to stay in prison and use the appellate process to get to Rome. Paul was able to interpret his vision to get to Rome through the circumstance of being in prison. He seized that opportunity to fulfill God's mission on his life.

Although John was never jailed for his beliefs, he did find lessons for his own sense of mission from Paul's experience. "The book of Acts reads like a war journal," John said, comparing it to his battlefield experience. "Most of the Congressional Medals of Honor are awards on behalf of the issue of courage. It's clear from the book of Acts that once a Christian is captured by Christ, that person is not captured to be a spectator. He or she is invited out of the stadium and onto the playing field of everyday life. The church is the hope of the world. It is not only the hope of the world, it is *the only hope* of the world." John knew beyond a shadow of a doubt that he had to take that message to his "Rome"—Moscow, the capital of the communist world.

Just as Paul was to become the apostle to the Gentiles and had a date with Rome, John became an apostle to countries in bondage to communism and had a date with Moscow. Moscow was the Rome of the communist world. At its peak, communism controlled more than forty nations across Europe, Asia, Africa, and the Caribbean. The geography of the communist world dwarfed the geography of the Roman Empire several times over. And John's apostleship would take him throughout all the communist world—from Europe to Asia to Latin America in the Western Hemisphere.

When we consider the scope of John's impact through East-West, what he and the ministry accomplished is staggering. During a twenty-five-year period, 191 million people had the gospel presented to them, 190,000 churches were planted, and 1.26 million leaders were trained. Just as God used Paul to transform the cities of Western Asia, the

Mediterranean, and Europe, God would use John to impact multitudes of people across the breadth of the communist world.

JOHN'S CALL TO MOSCOW

After John returned from Vietnam, he met Jody Dillow through mutual friends in Dallas. Jody was studying ministry at Dallas Theological Seminary, and they quickly became friends and got together regularly to play racquetball or go jogging. More importantly, though, they both wanted to be on the cutting edge of God's work and were dreaming big dreams. As they jogged, they visualized building a team of commando Christians whom they could place in difficult parts of the world to introduce and open that area to the gospel.

Whenever John thought about or discussed the possibility of reaching people in communist countries, his heart beat more quickly. Being in Vietnam had opened his eyes to how desperately those populations needed freedom—not just physical but, more importantly, the spiritual freedom Christ offers. He was all in and wanted to be part of that movement, which he knew God was orchestrating.

After Jody graduated seminary, he moved to Vienna, Austria, while John continued working in Dallas in the business community as well as sharing the gospel with the athletes at Southern Methodist University and other places. Though distance now kept them from jogging or playing racquetball, they continued to connect regularly on those dreams and how to make them realities.

Not long after Jody began ministering in Vienna, he became part of a consortium of mission organizations that banded together to pursue the same dreams Jody and John had discussed on those many jogs. Agencies such as Campus Crusade, Navigators, Slavic Gospel, Open Doors, and Conservative Baptists all came around the table.

Jody contacted John with the news and invited him to an initial meeting the consortium was holding in Vienna. The topic was taking the gospel behind the Iron Curtain.[4] The question at hand was, "What is the greatest need behind the Iron Curtain?" They quickly realized that nobody was training the next generation of Christian leaders.

The agencies asked Jody if he would be their point person to begin setting their plans in place. They committed to invest financially to create an underground training movement of leaders. Jody turned to John to partner with him in this task. When John would go to Europe for business, he would fly through Vienna to visit Jody. They began to talk and dream about training and setting up this underground school behind the Iron Curtain.

By this point John had more freedom in his work to travel internationally with Jody to build out a network of Christian leaders behind the Iron Curtain. What looked like mere coincidence was God using this timing to converge His plans for John and for those communist countries.

The dreams that John and Jody had shared together on those many jogs began to take shape as the organizations in the consortium provided different people to be on staff with the training school. The spirit of the consortium was that everyone wanted to pool resources and personnel to have a robust training institution. The members of the consortium built a team and began training indigenous leaders in communist countries.

The team began to set up underground networks to train the next generation of Christian leaders. John focused primarily on Russia. He began to travel and secretly set up his network in the country and worked to make connections in Romania. As he met with more and more leaders, they asked him to come and engage with them there, so he would meet with and teach the Bible to leaders in the underground church.

John's date with Moscow was set. And he stood at the crossroads of closing the chapter in the business world and pursuing a full-time focus on training the next generation of leaders behind the Iron Curtain.

CHAPTER 4

TWO SPEECHES AT MOSCOW STATE UNIVERSITY

God was preparing the world for a cataclysmic confrontation between the truths of democracy and the despair of communism, between the freedom that comes with belief versus the spiritual bondage of atheism. For one, God prepared and used President Ronald Reagan. For the other, He prepared and used John Maisel.

The Cold War was in full effect. From the 1950s through the 1980s, Russia had been at a fierce ideological and military standoff with the United States. The Bay of Pigs fiasco of 1963, the nuclear-arms buildup, and the political stalemate were all reminders of the intensity of the relationship between the two nations. And by the mid-1980s, President Reagan was ready for the standoff to end.

Journalist Bret Baier described it well in *Three Days in Moscow*:

The year 1984 dawned with a standoff between the Soviet Union and the United States, captured in *Time* magazine's "Men of the Year" cover on January 2, which showed a somber—even angry—illustration of Reagan and Andropov facing away from each other. "In the beginning were the words," the cover story began, describing the growing antagonism between the men. At the top, verbal missiles fired in magisterial wrath: Ronald Reagan denouncing the Soviet Union as an "evil empire" that had committed a "crime against humanity" when its fighters shot down a Korean jetliner; Yuri Andropov responding that the Reagan Administration had "finally dispelled" all "illusions" that it could be dealt with. At a baser level, crude vilification: American caricatures of Andropov as a "mutant from outer space."[1]

Yuri Andropov was the fourth General Secretary of the Soviet Union following the eighteen-year tenure of Leonid Breshniv. He was in his role for only fifteen months, until his sudden death in 1984. This coincided with the beginning of Ronald Reagan's second presidential term. The Soviet Union had an interim leader, Konstantin Chernanko, in 1984 before Mikhail Gorbachev became chairman in 1985.

Two men of humble roots and optimistic dispositions were fated to change the world: Mikhail Gorbachev and Ronald Reagan. This change represented an opportunity to create a new conversation about the future of the American-Soviet relationship.

Mikhail Gorbachev grew up in a Soviet Union where poverty and near famine were constants, even after the war, but none of that got Gorbachev down. "We were poor, practically beggars. But in general I felt wonderful," he said of his childhood.[2]

Also like Reagan, Gorbachev came from a family that was not well educated, but he craved learning and achieved the seemingly impossible goal of getting accepted into Moscow State University. There he joined the Communist Party but distinguished himself as something of an outsider and independent thinker.[3]

Between 1985 and 1988, President Reagan and Secretary Gorbachev met four times at four different summits. They met in Geneva, Reykjavik (Iceland), Washington DC, and Moscow. During these meetings they hammered out important agreements between the two nations—including the Intermediate-Range Nuclear Forces, or INF, Treaty document signed in 1987, and the Strategic Arms Reduction Treaty, which was eventually signed in 1991 by President George H. W. Bush. These negotiations reduced ballistic missiles by 50 percent, making the world a far safer place as the two countries focused on the themes of human rights and economic growth rather than mutual mass destruction.

President Reagan's leadership and his unexpected friendship with Secretary Gorbachev created the environment for the collapse of communism. In May 1988, during the final year of his presidency, President Reagan gave the penultimate speech of his life at Moscow State University, Gorbachev's alma mater.

In that setting, in front of a 1,200-strong communist audience, President Reagan said,

> Standing here before a mural of your revolution, I want to talk about a very different revolution that is taking place right now; quietly sweeping the globe without bloodshed or conflict. Its effects are peaceful, but they will fundamentally alter our world, shatter old assumptions, and reshape our lives. It's easy to underestimate because it's not accompanied by banners or fanfare. It's been called the technological or information revolution, and as its emblem, one might take the tiny silicon chip, no bigger than a fingerprint. One of these chips has more computing power than a roomful of old-style computers. . . .
>
> We Americans make no secret of our belief in freedom. . . . Go to any American town, to take just an example, and you'll see dozens of churches, representing many different beliefs—in many places, synagogues and mosques—and you'll see families of every conceivable nationality worshiping together. Go into any schoolroom, and there you will see children being taught the Declaration of Independence, that they are endowed by their Creator with certain unalienable rights—among them life, liberty, and the pursuit of happiness—that no government can justly deny; the guarantees in their Constitution for freedom of speech, freedom of assembly, and freedom of religion. . . .

Let me cite one of the most eloquent contemporary passages on human freedom. It comes, not from the literature of America, but from this country, from one of the greatest writers of the 20th century, Boris Pasternak, in the novel *Dr. Zhivago*. He wrote: "I think that if the beast who sleeps in man could be held down by threats—any kind of threat, whether of jail or of retribution after death—then the highest emblem of humanity would be the lion tamer in the circus with his whip, not the prophet who sacrificed himself. But this is just the point—what has for centuries raised man about the beast is not the cudgel, but an inward music—the irresistible power of unarmed truth."[4]

God had providentially been preparing President Reagan to give that speech in that year, 1988, in that city, Moscow, the capital of communism. This was not unlike Paul speaking in the city of Ephesus in the town hall of Tyrannus (see Acts 19:9-10). Because of Paul's work there, all of Asia heard the gospel within two years. Likewise, the entire communistic world heard the music of freedom in the song of President Reagan's speech.

Only 527 days after the Moscow State University speech, the Berlin Wall collapsed. The Berlin Wall, built after World War II, was significant, because it prevented people from traveling from communist East Germany to West Germany, which was free and democratic. The Berlin Wall was the global symbol of communism and its commitment to keep its citizens entrapped in its bankrupt political system. Its fall was the beginning of the end for the Cold War and the Iron Curtain.

Between November 9, 1989, and December 31, 1991, communism collapsed in Poland, East Germany, Czechoslovakia, Romania, and Albania—all strongholds in the Soviet Union. Each country's citizens took part in massive protests to demand reforms. Secretary Gorbachev refused to send in the military to prop up communistic governments. The music of freedom was preparing hearts to hear the song of ultimate freedom.

A NEW OPPORTUNITY TO SHARE THE GOSPEL

As John and the others were working underground with secret believers and praying for doors to open behind the Iron Curtain, they were still under great threat, because the police in those countries were watching them and their movements. That didn't deter them or their work, however, because the believers in these countries had a great hunger to be trained and encouraged in their faith. But the work was slow because of the dangers. When the Iron Curtain collapsed, however, everything changed for believers there, and John and the team had unprecedented opportunities to share the gospel.

One of those opportunities came at none other than Moscow State University.

After the collapse of the Berlin Wall in 1989, invitations went out to American businessmen in communist contexts to speak about their experiences and insight. Businesses throughout Russia had an enormous hunger for their businessmen to learn from their American compatriots.

John had been an important leader in the Co-Mission, which represented a consortium of agencies that had recognized the huge need for training Christian leaders behind the Iron Curtain before communism had fallen. John had been able to travel freely in and out of the former Soviet countries when the Iron Curtain was still up, because of his background as a businessman, even though his work was part of the underground movement. Since John was known throughout the area and had been working in Russia, leaders at Moscow State University invited him to lecture there on the topics of business and capitalism. He agreed to do so on one condition: he wanted to give a lecture on Christianity.

The Russians were not enthused about the condition, but John insisted. After several rounds of "negotiations," they gave in to his request.

On May 5, 1991, John stood in the same Moscow State University 1,200-seat auditorium as Reagan and presented his lecture, "Is Jesus God?" to more than seven hundred students, faculty, and Who's Who of Moscow.

With John's permission,[5] I include it here.

A person is born, and they go to school, have a family, continue to work, retire, and then die. Is this all there is to life? There must be something more to life than this, but where do we go from here?

What is our purpose? What is our destiny? How can we

be fulfilled and have the emptiness of our lives filled with true meaning?

The big question in the world today is, Who is Jesus Christ? This is why I have chosen to break down our journey into two questions:

(1) Is Jesus God?

(2) How can we know Him personally?

If we gathered religious experts from all over the world from different faiths and different backgrounds and we asked them, "Who is God?" we would have many different definitions. Some would say God is personal. Some would say that God is impersonal. But if we believe that truth is not relative, we would have to conclude that God cannot be both personal and impersonal at the same time.

Even when a person says there is no God, that person violates a basic philosophical principle. He is a person with a finite understanding making an absolute statement about the nature of infinity. It would be like asking how much total knowledge mankind possesses.

Albert Einstein, the Nobel Prize winner in physics, has said that mankind grasps less than one percent of total knowledge. If we have only one percent of total knowledge, would it not be possible for God to exist in the other 99 percent?

You can see that it is impossible for a person with a finite mind to make an absolute statement that there is no God because to do so one would need to possess total knowledge. Therefore, it is very difficult for people to think about what God is really like and be confident that their opinions are correct.

This is where we must start, with the question, Is there sufficient evidence for me to conclude that there is a God, and that I can have a personal relationship with Him? . . .

Let me stop right here to say that Jesus is unique among worldwide religious figures in His claim to be God. Buddha never claimed to be God. Moses never claimed to be Jehovah. Mohammed never claimed to be Allah. Yet Jesus Christ claimed to be the True and Living God!

The record shows that Jesus was not crucified because He raised the dead or because He made the blind to see and the lame to walk. Jesus was crucified because He claimed to be God. That makes the question of His deity of utmost importance. . . .

Your decision about Jesus Christ is more important than your ideology. It is more important than your career. And it is more important than the mate you choose. If Jesus is God, then you must decide what to do with that information. If He is not God, then we should have nothing to do with Him.

C. S. Lewis, formerly a professor at Oxford University, was an atheist who later became a Christian. In his writing, Lewis emphasized that one cannot be neutral with Jesus Christ. Lewis wrote:

> *I am trying here to prevent anyone saying the really foolish thing that people often say about Him: "I'm ready to accept Jesus as a great moral teacher, but I don't accept His claim to be God." That is the one thing we must not say. A man who was merely a man and said the sort of things Jesus said would not be a great*

moral teacher, He would either be a lunatic—on the level with a man who says he is a poached egg—or else He would be the Devil of Hell. You must make your choice. Either this man was, and is, the Son of God: or else a madman or something worse. You can shut Him up for a fool, you can spit at Him and kill Him as a demon; or you can fall at His feet and call Him Lord and God. But let us not come with any patronizing nonsense about His being a great human teacher. He has not left that open to us. He did not intend to.[6]

I hope that when you have finished hearing this, you will not continue to say that Jesus was just a good man. If you wish to be honest in the interest of intellectual integrity you cannot assume neutral ground. Jesus is either God or He is a liar. You may conclude that Jesus is not God and choose to dismiss Him, but as Professor Lewis said, please do not say He was just a good moral leader.

Jesus is the most unique personality the world has ever known. Jesus is not simply a great man among men. He's the greatest man who has ever lived. The more you study His life, the more you are impressed. Even atheists and skeptics acknowledge the uniqueness of Jesus. Listen to what the skeptics of the world have said about Jesus. . . .

Jesus Christ, according to the skeptics and people who knew His life, is considered the most unique person who has ever lived. Remember our question, "Who does the world say that Jesus Christ is?" Some people say that Jesus was legend or a myth, that He never really existed. Historian Phillip Schaff said, "The certainty of Jesus Christ is as certain as my own identity."

Tacitus, the Roman historian of the first century, spoke in detail of the person of Christ. Flavius Josephus, the well-known first-century Jewish historian, spoke of the life and death of Jesus and how He went about claiming to be the Messiah and performing great works.

Thanks to bibliographical testing, experts confirm the authenticity of documents by Caesar, Plato, Aristotle, and Tacitus and the reliability of their authorship. Let us apply the same test to biblical writings, to New Testament documents. The books of the New Testament were written from about AD 40 to AD 90. The earliest manuscript copies date from AD 130 to only forty to fifty years after the originals. More than thirteen thousand copies exist. Applying the bibliographical test of veracity to the New Testament, therefore, should make us think twice before we say that biblical literature cannot be trusted. When we apply the internal and external tests, one will see even more clearly why the Bible is a reliable document and definitely inspired by God.

The New Testament Greek scholar J. Harold Greenlee adds: "Since scholars accept as generally trustworthy the writings of the ancient classics even though the earliest manuscripts were written so long after the original writings and the number of exact manuscripts is in many instances so small, it is clear that the reliability of the text of the New Testament is assured."

Writers like Leo Tolstoy and others of your country (the USSR) have described the work of God's Spirit in utterly transforming their lives. Leo Tolstoy lived much of his life as an atheist but made this statement toward the end of his life: "For

35 years of my life I was, in the proper acceptation of the word, a nihilist—not a revolutionary socialist, but a man who believed in nothing. Five years ago, my faith came to me. I believed in the doctrine of Jesus, and my life underwent a sudden transformation—life and death ceased to be evil. Instead of despair, I tasted joy and happiness that death could not take away."

William Shakespeare, before his death said, "I commit my soul into the hands of God, my Creator, most assuredly believing in Jesus Christ, my Savior."

Today in the Soviet Union, Dr. Dmitry A. Kuznetsuv, a biochemist who has three earned doctorates, has won the Lenin Komsomol Prize in Science. He was in the United States in 1989 and spoke of his faith in Christ. He has also written an article in the Soviet Union on science. . . .

Let's go to the second question, "Who do you say that Jesus Christ is?"

Before you can answer that question, you need some evidence and facts that will help you make an intelligent decision. We must ask ourselves if there is sufficient evidence to warrant an intelligent belief in Jesus Christ as the Savior of the world. You see, my heart cannot do something that my mind rejects. Before we are through, you will have to answer the question, "Who is Jesus Christ?" with your heart. Many times in my own experience I have encountered some mental obstacles that had to be worked through before my faith could have the intelligent foundation that God desires. If God is there and not silent—if Jesus Christ is the answer to the needs of the human heart—God wants me to understand with my mind His plan to bring man into a relationship with Himself.

Christianity is built upon the solid foundation of knowing and being able to substantiate the claims of Jesus Christ. . . .

Thomas, the disciple who had doubted that Jesus really had risen from the dead, responded, "My Lord and my God" when he saw Jesus and felt the wounds in His hands and side (John 20:28).

After Jesus had raised a man from the dead, "He said, 'I am the resurrection and the life. He who believes in Me will live even if he dies'" (John 11:25, NASB).

Jesus did not say, "I am a way," He said, "I am the way." A lot of people think that God is sitting on the top of some mountain, and the people of the world have all these different ways to climb up this mountain and get to God who lives on top. They think that it really does not make any difference how they get up to the top where God is because everyone is climbing to get to the same place where they can know God.

The Muslim says, "Jesus was just a prophet, He was a good moral man. But He did not die on the cross, and He did not rise again on the third day. To get to God one must obey Mohammed." The Christian agrees with Jesus who said He is the Savior of the world. The Christian believes that Jesus died on the cross and three days later rose again from the dead. Both of these positions cannot be true. One is wrong, or they are both wrong. Furthermore, Jesus said, "I am the way," not "a way." That is an exclusive statement.

I did not come to you with that statement. Jesus said it. If there exists any other path to God other than through Jesus Christ, then Christ's death on the cross loses all meaning.

Does that seem narrow? Exclusive? Rigid? Perhaps so, but

God said it clearly and with no ambiguity because it is very important. No matter who we are, the best of us morally have fallen short of the perfection of God's standards. Because of our sin we are completely separated from God who loves us.

The emptiness and aloneness we have is because we are separated from the One who made us. He alone can give us peace, purpose, and joy for living. . . .

Jesus said He is the bridge that brings a holy God and a sinful mankind together. This is why Jesus Christ died. That is why the cross of Christ is the focal point of human history. The New Testament say in 1 Timothy 2:5-6: "There is one God and one mediator between God and man, the man Christ Jesus, who gave Himself as a ransom for all men, the testimony given at the proper time" (NASB).

If Jesus is the way, then none of these ways leads us to God:

New Age
Islam
Buddhism
Hinduism
Transcendentalism
Meditation
Psychic Phenomena

That is why reaching God requires more than a random path up a mountain. We can never offer God perfection—the mountain cannot be scaled. God said that He alone determined how people would come into His house. Jesus said, "I am the Way. I am the Door, and entering the Door takes you into God's house."

A WONDROUS RESPONSE

The lecture was scheduled to be an hour but lasted more than three hours. As John drew to the end of his message, he challenged those persons who wanted to embrace Jesus as God and commit their lives to Him to stand. It was an audacious request, given the environment in which John was presenting these bold claims. And yet more than one hundred students and faculty rose to their feet across the auditorium.

Two of the faculty who stood were Valentina, an English professor, and Professor T, who taught economics. Valentina was married to a KGB agent who had been spying on John. (John learned later that the KGB had set up three traps to determine if he was a foreign spy.)

When John finished his speech, he could feel the intense electricity remain in the room as the listeners gave him a standing ovation. Many of the leaders and professors wanted private meetings to talk more about his message. The momentum for change had begun.

Through John's words, the Holy Spirit lit a fuse in the lives of people that day, a fuse that would result in planting churches in Moscow. Valentina and Professor T were instrumental in planting the Church of the Word of Christ in Moscow.

But the movement didn't stop in Moscow. Another man, Gwang Lu from China, was in the audience that day and also was converted to Christianity after listening to John's message. He was so motivated by the power of his spiritual transformation that he attended Dallas Theological

Seminary and then returned to his country to share the gospel with others.

The foundation for the creation of a new ministry to reach the darkest places around the globe had been set.

CHAPTER 5

FROM MOSCOW
TO THE WORLD

John Maisel gave his "Is Jesus God?" speech on May 5, 1991, at Moscow State University, almost exactly three years after President Ronald Reagan made his speech in the identical location. Just as with the impact Reagan's speech had, no one had any idea of the catalytic impact John's speech would have.

The response was explosive. John saw immediately that Russia had a tremendous need for believers to plant churches and to train pastors to lead those churches. So in 1993, with a passion to make disciples in all nations and a vision for starting a new ministry, John contacted a good friend and colleague, Bud Toole, whom he had gotten to know well in the early 1980s when John first started talking about a possible ministry effort in the Soviet Union. Bud had been so motivated by the possibilities that he came out of the business world—he'd been a money manager and involved on Wall Street for several years—and moved with his wife, Carolyn, to Vienna to get involved with the Vienna consortium.

Though John had been working for more than a decade traveling throughout communist countries and consulting with other mission organizations, he felt the call to do more. As John shared his dream, Bud, along with several others, immediately came on board. That year, they launched East-West Ministries. East-West would rise to meet that call as a mission organization with a zeal for empowering national pastors and local believers to transform their communities in the spiritually darkest places by making disciples and multiplying churches.

Under John's leadership, their goals were to (1) mobilize the body of Christ by training and sending believers from various backgrounds across cultures to reach the unreached and start church-planting movements; (2) evangelize the lost by using simple, biblical, and reproducible tools that their missionaries and national partners could use to invite the lost into a relationship with Jesus Christ; and (3) equip local believers by empowering them with simple tools to share the gospel, disciple new believers, and strategically plant churches in their own contexts.

As East-West began reaching out to potential partners, investors and intercessors saw the historic potential to reach into the darkest corners of the globe. Partners were attracted by John's passion and their mutual love for their Savior and commitment to the Great Commission.

Today, twenty-five years after its inception, East-West is still going strong. East-West missionaries and national partners have planted more than 190,000 churches across fifty countries in ten regions of the world, including Africa, Russia and the Caucasus, Central Asia, East Asia, South Asia, Southeast Asia, the Middle East, Latin America, Europe, and North America. They are currently working under a three-year vision to multiply one million new disciples in the world's spiritually darkest areas.

THE EXPLOSIVE GROWTH OF EAST-WEST'S EXPANSION

John had worked throughout the Soviet Union, and its arms stretched around the world, yet his idea for East-West came in 1990 by way of India through a businessman who was originally from Bangalore, India. They met while the man was attending Dallas Theological Seminary. The man encouraged John to plant churches and train leaders in the darkest places of the globe. The man and his mission impressed John and stuck in his mind as he formed East-West.

One of this newly birthed ministry's first endeavors was to plant a church in the heart of the former Soviet Union— Moscow. The response to the church plant was tremendous, including from several prominent faculty at Moscow State University.

Holding John's same ideal of the urgency of "today and that day," East-West's next focus continued to expand throughout the region. And by 1995, their work training leaders and birthing churches included several other locations, including the closed country of Kazakhstan in central

Asia. East-West was finding great receptivity in the former Soviet republics in central Asia.

By 1997, East-West had penetrated Latin America, which opened as a mission field. Over the next twenty years, it would become the most visited short-term mission field for East-West. By 2016, forty short-term mission trips were being taken annually to Latin America. East-West had firmly planted itself in the Western Hemisphere.

Since East-West's vision is to take the gospel into the hardest and darkest places, in 2003, they began their work in Asia, planting churches in Buddhist countries. For instance, Myanmar had experienced the Saffron Revolution of 2017 when the price of fuel escalated by 100 percent. Since East-West had demonstrated an ability to work with Christian communities in oppressive countries, they saw the opportunity to take advantage of the opening and sent workers to share the gospel with the citizens there who had felt economic and spiritual oppression. And the citizens responded.

Next they turned their sights toward other Asian countries, which represent approximately one-third of the global population.

In Europe, East-West planted its works throughout several unreached nations between 2011 and 2015. These unnamed countries range from 0.3 percent evangelical to an atheist country to a country that is 98 percent Muslim.

Most recently, East-West established itself in Paris, considered the third-most-influential city in the world after London and New York.

EAST-WEST'S TRAINING STRATEGY

The vision of East-West has always been to train disciples and to multiply churches. In 2005, East-West had thirty men in its first training cohort in one Southeast Asian country. Men were trained to plant churches and to multiply that training.

In 2007, the model shifted as training centers funded by Americans were closed and replaced with an indigenous, national-led training model. This model has spread throughout the globe in the East-West methodology.

By 2014, East-West established Extreme Team Mission trips. Local guides lead short-term missionaries on rough terrain "hikes," carrying only their backpacks, through regions in the Himalayan Mountains where they share the gospel with people living in remote villages.

East-West also initiates and oversees other short-term mission trips to such regions as Latin America, Asia, and Africa. These trips are often the first experience for young people as well as senior marketplace leaders to openly share their faith. This is especially meaningful because many of the people they share with have never heard the Good News.

WHY EAST-WEST MINISTRIES HAS THRIVED

East-West Ministries began to have a global impact, much greater than John or the others had initially imagined. It moved beyond the borders of the former Soviet Union and found itself in some of the other darkest areas of the world as well. Consider some of the many accomplishments they've seen:

- 1985: John traveled behind the Iron Curtain for the first time.
- 1991: John presented the gospel to former Soviets at Moscow State University.
- 1993: East-West was established.
- 1995: East-West expanded beyond its work in Russia.
- 1997: East-West created a plan to mobilize believers to put their faith into action.
- 2003: East-West began ministry vision to share the gospel with fifty million people in ten years.
- 2007: East-West launched church-planting movement strategies on the mission field.
- 2010: John stepped down from full-time work to act as chairman emeritus, and Kurt Nelson became chief executive officer and president.
- 2013: East-West began the work to implement a vision to multiply one million disciples in five years.
- 2018: Over its twenty-five year history, God used East-West to reach more than 191 million people with the gospel, seeing 1.83 million disciples made, training more than 1.26 million leaders, and planting more than 190,000 house churches.[1]

God's work through John and East-West is impressive. But why and how did it become so successful? These three primary factors had much to do with it.

Factor #1: *The Spirit of God Freshly Moving Across the Planet*

John's leadership in founding East-West did not happen in a vacuum. The Spirit of God was moving in remarkable ways over several decades, which resulted in tremendous breakthrough into new contexts. John's leadership in the darkest places on the planet are directly connected to an emerging global prayer movement.

The 1980s, 1990s, and early 2000s saw unprecedented gatherings of prayer across the globe. Whether it be one million gathered in South Korea, stadium events across Indonesia, or the Global Day of Prayer phenomena involving fifty million followers of Jesus, people are heeding the call to action through prayer—and God is answering. Jim Denison, cofounder of Denison Forum on Truth and Culture, has said that more Muslims have become Christian in the past fifteen years than in the previous 1,500 years. That is a remarkable spiritual answer to prayer.

The global prayer movement has been a powerful companion to the courageous evangelism taking place in the ten regions and nearly fifty nations impacted by East-West. Indonesia is the largest Muslim nation on the planet yet may have the most organized national prayer movement in the world. India, the epicenter of Hinduism, has had highly organized city gospel movements across the subcontinent.

Though it is just one expression of the global church at prayer, the Global Day of Prayer is illustrative of how God is stirring. In 2001, more than forty-five thousand Christians united for a Day of Repentance and Prayer at Newlands Stadium in Cape Town. In 2002, Christians in South Africa gathered in eight different venues for a Day of Repentance and Prayer. On May 1, 2003, seventy-seven South-African regions and twenty-seven African countries committed to a Day of Repentance and Prayer for Africa.

In May 2004, history was made when Christians from all fifty-six nations of Africa participated in the first-ever continental Day of Repentance and Prayer for Africa. In South Africa, 277 communities participated.

In May 2005, Christians from 156 of 220 nations of the world united across denominational and cultural borders for the first Global Day of Prayer. In 2008, millions of Christians from 214 nations united in prayer, and on May 31, 2009, a miracle happened when the initiative miraculously expanded to two hundred countries in the world.

May 2010 saw the ten-year celebration of the Global Day of Prayer. While Christians from around the world united in prayer in Cape Town, where everything started, millions from 220 nations once again gathered in their own nations.

The fact that South Africa was the womb for this global prayer movement was not accidental. Christians prayed and acted to bring about a bloodless revolution in the transition from apartheid to a democratic government in 1994.[2]

Looking back and seeing God's hand reveals clearly the relationship between the explosive growth of East-West and the dynamic power of prayer around the world. God heard and answered. New frontiers of evangelism were forged, even as a powerful expression of prayer was established around the globe.

Factor #2: John Maisel's Leadership

To birth a movement of this magnitude, its leader requires particular character traits—traits that John has developed, grown, and exhibited consistently throughout his life and work.

Intimacy with Jesus. John tries to spend at least one hour or more a day focusing on the Scriptures and praying them back to the Father as he goes through his day. From his perspective, every encounter with anyone about anything is a "divine appointment."

As he meets with work colleagues, friends, and others, he often talks with them about what he is learning from his time in the Bible. John is extraordinarily grounded in the truth of Jesus. He can teach from the Scriptures to three to four men's marketplace groups every week, because the well of his spiritual intimacy with Jesus is so deep.

A sharp sense of the eternal. As we discussed previously, this eternal view was deepened within him in a profound way during his time in Vietnam. John saw many young men in their twenties die on the battlefield. While there he had made life-and-death choices based on his understanding of whether or not his men were ready to meet their Maker.

For more than forty years, John has maintained the discipline of seizing every opportunity to share the gospel in every situation that affords itself. John is an initiator, as evidenced in his days as an athlete, soldier, and business leader. These skills have served him well as a missionary statesman with East-West.

Knowing God in a way that expresses itself with extraordinary boldness. Theologian J. I. Packer wrote that people who know their God are people who have great boldness for God, great energy to pray, and great contentment in God.³ Anyone who has spent more than a time or two with John will experience his passion to share the gospel with others—waiters, the homeless, security guards, gym attendants, senior marketplace leaders, and young people. On his last trip to a Latin American country in 2018, he needed to wear a mask because of the air pollution affecting his lungs. Yet there he was on the streets of the country's most populated city, sharing the gospel with anyone who would listen. Nothing deterred him from sharing with boldness his knowledge about God.

One of the remarkable dynamics regarding East-West and John's never-ending boldness and pursuit of his calling is that John was fifty-three years old when the mission began. Historically most mission movements are started by leaders under the age of twenty-eight. In many ways, John is a Caleb figure, who after forty years of waiting in the wilderness was eager to fight for his Promised Land inheritance in Canaan (see Joshua 14:6-15).

Being present with others. When you are with John, you are with John. What makes his witnessing so credible is that he engages with that person. He is concerned about that person. He is not distracted by what is happening around him. He doesn't engage half-heartedly with his attention focused on his phone or on other things.

An infectious faith. John's faith is infectious. One of the reasons East-West has grown so extraordinarily is because others want to join a mission that transcends the routines of going to church and having a faith that doesn't require any risk. Everyone wants to do something historically significant. Participating with John and East-West has been a way for people to live out their grander purposes.

Over the past twenty-five years, thousands of spiritually mighty men and women have joined the East-West movement. This community of leaders has included career missionaries, short-term missionaries, board members, support staff, and a generous investor community. At the core of the movement has been John's spirited, relentless passion to share Jesus with everyone.

Factor #3: The Christian Marketplace Community of Dallas

As we looked at earlier in the book, God did something remarkable in Dallas in 1972. Emerging from Explo '72 and the hundreds of thousands of young evangelists at that Dallas gathering, the fuse had been lit to catalyze Christians in the city. Since then, Dallas continues to thrive as it continues to catalyze leaders, making Dallas the "Antioch of America" with its commitment to missions. (Antioch was the base of operations for Paul and Barnabas. See Acts 13).

The sovereign, supernatural work that God was stirring in Dallas would lay an important foundation for the future establishment of East-West twenty-one years later. That foundation of a praying, giving, going marketplace community would help propel the rapid growth of East-West.

From my observations after traveling the globe to thirty-three major cities, today Dallas has more megachurches than any other city in the world. After Singapore, many believe Dallas has the highest concentration of Christian marketplace leader talent in the world.

Many boards of great organizations throughout the Dallas area have strategically used this concentration of talent to help lead as well as to provide the financial capital to share the gospel with the world. Organizations and movements like East-West, Dallas Theological Seminary, Salvation Army, and Dallas Baptist University are a small sample of world-class leadership in Dallas. East-West is at the forefront of pioneering an aggressive commitment to church planting in the darkest places.

Dallas is a burgeoning economic engine that has evolved into a cultural, political, educational, and entertainment center on a global scale. Its two major airports serve fifty-six global destinations daily, with Beijing being the most recently added direct nonstop destination. The emergence of East-West under John's leadership has paralleled the growth of Dallas as an economic and transportation center.

The backbone of East-West is a committed core of Christian marketplace leaders. They have an extraordinary loyalty to advancing the gospel of Jesus, as well as to John Maisel and to the current CEO, Kurt Nelson. The participation and generosity of this core group has fueled the movement to impact the most-challenged regions of the world. And it all began when God entrusted John with a vision for global ministry and John took that vision, partnered with Bud Toole, and founded East-West.

As John likes to remind us: God's work done God's way will always have God's presence. As God allowed John to launch His work around the globe, passing the baton of leadership to Kurt Nelson and the East-West team, He continues to advance the gospel in the darkest areas of the world at this unique time in history. As John tells the team at East-West, "The past twenty-five years have been nothing more than preparation for what God wishes to do in the future. Yes, the best is still in front for all God has called to hear the truth of the gospel. Jesus plus nothing equals everything."

John and Susie on their wedding day, January 21, 1961

John's official
Marines photo

Passing out gospel resources in Russia

Handing out Bibles
in Russia

Speaking to
Russian locals

At a Russian gospel outreach event

Preparing to speak at a Russian gospel outreach event

With a literature distribution team, preparing material
for overseas mission work

In Moscow, teaching the Bible with a group of men whom he led to Jesus

Speaking in Kiev at an evangelistic outreach.
When so many people attended to hear John speak,
Franklin Graham went to the next outreach and spoke there.

Baptizing a Jewish
woman he led to the Lord

A Tribute To My Father

One of my most treasured possessions is a photograph of me and you. I believe in the picture we were dancing at my wedding reception. Every time I look at it, it makes me smile and it reminds me of the beautiful relationship I have with you. I am truly a very lucky girl to have a father like you.

I know the Lord knew what He was doing when He gave you to me as my dad. I have really needed a stabilizing factor in my life and besides the Lord, it has always been you. I am so thankful for John Maisel as my father and one of my most treasured friends. So.... on your "55th" birthday, I have written my own tribute to you.

First of all, I want to thank you for all of your support for my relationship with Harry. I was so afraid of getting married because I thought I wouldn't be "daddy's little girl" anymore but you proved me wrong. You have been wonderful in your support and been such an encouragement in my marriage and have always been there to share your wisdom but never intervene. You are still my "daddy" and I will always be your "little girl"

I want to thank you for being my personal "Prayer Warrior". I know that you and mom pray for me all the time and I know the prayers are what have guided me to make the right choices and decisions. Although not right all the time, you were always there to pray me out of my turmoil. I truly appreciate your prayers.

I also want to thank you for all of your wisdom. We have been down some tough roads together and your wisdom has always helped me get thru those rough spots. Your bible verses, counseling and example for Christ have impacted my life more than you will ever know. Thank you for your wisdom.

One of the most wonderful things about our relationship is that you are my friend. We have had many wonderful fun times together and laughed until we cried! Hardly a harsh word has ever been spoken between us. I know you will always be there... I am thankful you're my friend.

I want you to know you are absolutely the BEST! I love you more than anything and I am so blessed to have you in my life. You have impacted me in so many ways, and brought so many people to the Lord. Thank you for your example and courage to be a man that honors God always.

Here is to you and your undying love for me. Thank you for being my father and for being my friend, mentor and supporter. Happy "55th" Birthday and I look forward to many more wonderful years. I love you!

A'Dina 1995

Letter from John's daughter, A'Dina, to John

East-West Ministries first-ever staff retreat

At East-West Ministries' headquarters in Dallas

Speaking overseas with the use of a translator

Sharing spiritual
thoughts at the Dallas
Country Club

East-West board members, including many of the original board

Holding his most prized possession, his Bible, before sharing the gospel

Teaching the Bible

On a short-term mission trip in South Asia, 2010

East-West house church in South Asia, June 2010

Leadership, evangelism, and church planting training
in South Asia, June 2010

East-West Ministries event with President George W. Bush, March 3, 2012.
East-West's CEO, Kurt Nelson, left; John Maisel, right.

John speaking at East-West event with President George W. Bush, March 3, 2012

John with Valentina in Russia, August 2012; Valentina was the first believer to come to faith through East-West's ministry efforts

John with Joe Wall and Kurt Nelson in Russia, August 2012

Speaking with a believer in Russia, August 2012

John and Joe Wall meeting with pastors of a local Russian church,
August 2012. These men were led to faith and trained by John and Joe
in the early nineties, and their church is still going strong today!

East-West house church in Latin America, January 2013

On a trip in Vietnam, January 2016

East-West board, 2017

Mission trip to Latin America, May 2018

With Sam Spicer, a mission trip participant, sharing the gospel
with the local people in Latin America, May 2018

Morning Bible study with Latin
America short-term trip team,
May 2018

Mac Pier interviewing John Maisel in Washington DC
at the 100 City Summit

John, Susie, and their grandkids, Maxson and Nicole, 2018

PART TWO

JOHN'S MESSAGE

CHAPTER 6

THE NECESSITY OF COURAGE

As anyone who has interacted with John can attest, one of his greatest attributes is his courage. Not only on the battlefields in Vietnam or in the boardroom, it is through his unequivocal courage in introducing people to God every day. Then it is helping others go deeper in their faith and knowledge of God that matters most.

But what does John really think of courage? How does he define it and why does it matter? Perhaps the best way to answer those questions is to look at what he's written on that topic. Following are adaptations from his unpublished reflections.

WHAT DOES COURAGE LOOK LIKE?

We can see courage only in the context of attitude or action where context will determine whether courage was demonstrated. Jesus was courageous with silence when Pilate commanded Him to speak, but His silence was honoring to the Father. His willingness to "drink the cup" of His Father's will was courageous when He had the power to call ten thousand legions of angels but He didn't. As always for the Christian, Christ is the supreme model of our calling, which is to follow the attitude of *Yes, Father, I will obey no matter what.*

THE COURAGE OF ACTION

Let's break down this virtue of courage, this fruit of the Spirit that we as Christians have been called to live with in a hostile world—a world God desires to redeem and reconcile to Himself.

To lay a foundation related to pleasing God requires us to have true faith, which is faith seen in the outworking of courage. The reason we celebrate heroes of the faith is because we admire their courage. They "pull the trigger" on what they said they believed.

- Noah started preaching righteousness and building the ark, even though the earth had never experienced rain.
- Abraham left his home country and followed God's leading, even though he didn't know where he was going.
- Moses stood before the most powerful man on the face of the earth and gave him God's message.
- David ran to the battle when the opposition looked invincible.

We always see courage by our actions, not by what we say we believe.

FIRST PRINCIPLE OF COURAGE: THE ODDS ARE AGAINST YOU

As you look at each of the men and women of faith in Hebrews 11, it seems that God wants to put you in a place where the odds are always against you in doing what God wants you to do. God understands this because He intends to get involved when the odds are against us—but God won't appear unless we have stepped out first in the impossible.

Let's take a snapshot look at what God wants us to learn about courage when He asks us to do something and the odds are against us. We see a wonderful example in the story of Jonathan and his armor bearer.

We men need to relate to this story. It's a William Wallace "Braveheart" story about how we all want to "pick a fight" by the way we live, especially "pick a fight" that involves God's fight.

Jonathan and his armor bearer were on patrol one day watching for the Philistines who had taken up several strategic positions in Israel and were preparing for a big fight. The Philistines had all the weapons—strategic positions—and most of the men of Israel were scared to death. Even their leader, Saul, Jonathan's father, was hiding with all the rest. But not Jonathan and his buddy out on patrol; they were looking for a fight.

They came upon a threatening situation where most of us would offer excuses to run and hide. Not Jonathan. He was courageous. Look at his story in 1 Samuel 14.

Jonathan felt God prompting him to take on this group of Philistine soldiers—even though he was severely outnumbered. But Jonathan didn't consider the numbers, because they didn't matter to him. His response was an attitude of *Yes, Lord, no matter what,* and he engaged the enemy. As the result of his efforts, Jonathan defeated twenty Philistines. His courage was what made it possible for him to prevail, even though the odds were against him.

Think about this: they were outnumbered 20:2. That's 10:1 and those are not good odds for a fight. I had trouble in my early years with 1:1! But once again, what was Jonathan's perspective, his belief system?

It didn't make any difference if they won or lost, lived or died, succeeded or failed. Because he practiced living by the code of *Yes, Lord, no matter what.*

None of those things mattered. What mattered was that God would be honored, glorified, and magnified. It was about God, not about their safety, their comfort, their reputation, their success, their fame.

If you think Jonathan and his armor bearer's odds were scary, check some of these other odds where God was involved and His people courageously prevailed:

- Gideon's army of a mere three hundred stood against the Midianites' mighty army of thousands (Judges 6–7).
- Elijah stood alone against 450 priests of Baal (1 Kings 18).
- Jehoshaphat and a choir stood against a vast army of Edom, which included Moabites, Ammonites, and Meunites (2 Chronicles 20).

Now look at a few that had no numbers, but great odds against them:

- Abraham had a son at the age of one hundred.
- Moses stood against Pharaoh and the Egyptian army.
- David faced off against a Philistine giant.

You must understand that when God leads, usually the odds that you see with your eyes or feel with your emotions will tell you that you are facing an impossible situation. But it is *supposed* to be impossible when God asks you, because God intends to get involved in the process if you will act courageously—no matter what.

THE SECOND PRINCIPLE OF COURAGE: RISK IS ALWAYS INVOLVED

The second principle is this: risk is always involved. When the odds are against you, risk is a big part of the equation. Risk becomes a factor when there is no certainty of the outcome of your choice or actions.

Few things in life do not fall under the risk category, because we don't know how it will turn out. When we go into the hospital to have an operation, we must sign a waiver that states we understand the risks and if something goes wrong the hospital will not be held responsible.

We are all aware of the risk/reward factor in business decisions and stock choices. The greater the risk, the greater the reward. Every stock offering I have ever looked at states clearly on the first page and usually in bold print—**RISK FACTOR.**

If I buy the stock, I may make some money or I may lose money. If I have the operation, it may go well or it may not go well. If I buy a piece of land, the value may go up or it may go down. A risk is present because I don't know how it will turn out. As John Piper says, risk always contains the possibility of loss or injury as well as gain.

Everything involves a risk in one way or another. Hudson Taylor is credited to once have said, "Unless your exploitation for God contains an element of risk, most likely faith is not required." The dynamics of risk is present because we cannot control the outcome. When we step out in the spiritual realm especially, we have no control over future events. Think for a moment about how this might work in everyday life.

Something happens when you try a new job or start your own company. It may succeed or it may fail. You are at risk because you have no control over future events. Therefore Scripture teaches us that the ultimate outcomes must be in the hands of God and we can know He will ultimately use it for His purposes, if we have been obedient and moved by the desire to honor Him, no matter what. This is the type of faith that pleases God.

Let's say you are presented with an investment opportunity. As you begin to research the possibility you notice that on the first page is a statement that says, "Risk Factor." This statement reminds you of all the things that can go wrong with the investment. It's like a prescription drug—it does not tell you what it might do that is good for you, it only lists all the problems you may have if you take the drug. But let's say you have done your homework and you feel it is a worthy investment. You consider these factors:

- It is a risk, so you cannot know all that might happen. You can gain or you can lose.
- When you put your money in that deal, you lose control over all the events that can happen in a worldwide economy.
- You hope that you will gain a profit.

As a Christian, you have prayed about this decision, since you are a manager of the resources God has given you and sense the freedom to move ahead by faith. If you know you are not in control but God is in control, you rest in faith that may lead to a test of faith. The test of faith is when you do what God asks you to do but don't have the results that you had hoped for.

If it is an investment and you lose money instead of making money, the "no matter what" decision that started with a "Yes, Lord" must have confidence that God has a greater purpose for the loss that is greater than the gain. It will be for your good and for God's glory. Therefore Scripture asks us to have a heart attitude of gratitude for whatever the outcome may be.

A biblical illustration is Moses. He went to Pharaoh to have him release the Hebrew people. But Pharaoh rejected the request and gave a harsh penalty to the Hebrews by doubling their brick-making quota and forcing them to make bricks without straw. That resulted in Moses' people getting mad at him. They told Moses, "Leave us alone."

Moses was doing what God wanted him to do but he got an angry reaction that was not what he had hoped for. But God had a purpose by taking the straw away from the people. God was intensifying a "boot camp" for physical fitness to get the people ready for what lay ahead of them. This was a difficult time for Moses—facing the people's rejection— but this was where courage stepped in. The same with us: much of our faith will be tested in our walk with God when He leads us into callings that require risk.

THE THIRD PRINCIPLE OF COURAGE: HOPE IS THE MOTIVATING FACTOR

The third principle is that hope is the motivating factor of our willingness to take risks for God, which then leads to courageous living. There is no courage unless we have hope. This is the hope of faith. Hebrews 11:1 defines faith as the "confidence in what we hope for."

Hope is always a desire for gain. The question is, what is the desire for gain you hope for? If you have a surgical operation, you hope to gain better health. If you make an investment that has risk, you hope to gain a profit.

All our decisions that relate to our life of faith will have this hope. Hope is the focus on gain; what we ultimately desire to gain with our faith is important. We must be very clear on this hope of gain, as this hope is what will give meaning to the "no matter what."

Paul and our models in Scripture were driven not toward their own success, their reputation, their home, or their importance, but toward God's glory, His majesty, His honor,

His reputation, His fame, and drawing people toward Jesus Christ no matter what. They felt that whatever happened to them, as long as their actions brought honor to God, then they were pleased and content. The outcome was not what was important; their focus was on their hope that Christ had been magnified.

Hebrews 11 summarizes this perspective in verses 33 to 35 where we see those who succeeded and those who failed. Some good things resulted for those who took the risk by faith, having the hope that God would be honored. Some bad things happened to some who were just as pleasing to God. Their hope was not the visible outcome but the eternal outcome of God's glory. The bad, painful, or difficult things didn't matter to those who had those circumstances handed to them. Their ultimate hope was that their actions would result in Christ receiving the attention and glory due His name.

Peter Marshall is credited to have said, "I'd rather fail in that which will ultimately succeed than to succeed in that which will ultimately fail." Society measures success by results, but God measures success by faithfulness. In God's economy, we can treat our success with equity and our failures without regret, knowing that God's loving intent is that He can sometimes instruct us better through our failures than through our successes.

What we do by faith to the face of Jesus under the authority of Jesus and for the glory of Jesus will never involve failure from God's point of view. The key value goes back to this question: *Whom do I want to please—my Lord and God or my friends and peers?*

SAYING "YES, LORD, NO MATTER WHAT YOUR MISSION"

Risk, hope, and courage are the three elements we need in order to follow God's call. Let me offer a story that illustrates these principles clearly.

In Joshua 2, Joshua sent out spies into Jericho to see about taking the city. But the spies were detected and about to be compromised. They hid, and when Rahab discovered them, she was confronted with the decision of what to do. Her thinking might have followed this process that led to making the most important decision in her life.

Think about her situation. As a prostitute, over the years she probably picked up some bits and pieces of information from the camel caravans that would overnight outside Jericho. She probably heard some of the rumors about this Hebrew God by the name of Yahweh and some stories about how the Hebrew people were brought out of Egypt in such a powerful way. All she had were some hearsay and stories.

She had no Bible to check out.

She had no friend who could guide her in the ways of God.

She had no church prayer group or council.

All she had were rumors and a sense that the talk about this God was different from all the idols she had worshiped before. She made a decision to hide the spies and go with what little she knew about this Yahweh who had stirred her heart. She took about a "thimble full" of information, and with it she took a huge leap of faith.

She put everything on the table—her future, her family, her life, her assets, everything—and took the risk to say yes to this God, no matter what. God responded by putting her in the genealogy of Christ, His Son. She is listed in Hebrews 11 as a hero of the faith. She is used as an illustration of faith in James 2. She is found in the genealogy of Jesus in Matthew 1:5.

God made her a hero of the faith and uses her as an illustration of taking risk by faith when we have no control over the outcome.

This was a woman of courage. Against incredible odds, Rahab risked, because she had hope to gain God's blessing.

What was it that blessed the heart of God so much that He would use her and her story all these times in Scripture to illustrate a life of faith? Think about it.

Our problem today is that we have a huge amount of information, truth, and support, yet we take only a thimble's worth of risk.

Our culture says, "It's okay to believe whatever you wish, as long as your highest values in my 'belief system' are tolerance and 'political correctness.' You better not speak about Jesus." But our risk is more important, for our "biblical belief system" says the truth of Jesus Christ and God's love must be communicated no matter what the consequences to ourselves, our careers, our friends, or our social acceptance. The greater the consequence, the greater the courage needed to risk what we may lose if we act by faith upon our beliefs.

Do you really believe:

- Jesus is the way, the truth, the life?
- You are a citizen of heaven, not earth?

- God can be trusted no matter what happens related to your losses or gains?
- The truth of God's purposes as seen in the Bible are more important than your job or career or social acceptance?

If you really believe these to be true, then you will step out no matter what to confront your culture with the truth of God's love. If you believe this—and only what you *do* really determines what you believe—will you act courageously, regardless of the outcome, no matter what?

The heroes of faith in Hebrews 11 acted by faith with courage. They did so because their hopes to gain God's honor, glory, and blessing were where they found true happiness. They found true happiness not only for now but, more importantly, for eternity.

CHAPTER 7

TAKE A STAND—
NO MATTER WHAT

In 1989, the revolution began that overthrew the communist regime in Romania. It started with a Hungarian Reformed congregation in Timisoara. Practicing Christianity was against the law. Routinely, the secret police would have killed anyone they caught worshiping God, but they must have thought that killing this congregation's pastor, Laszlo Tokes, would have made him a martyr, potentially causing them even more trouble. Instead they opted to exile him to a small, remote village outside of Timisoara. A court ordered his eviction from his home and church, set to take place December 15, 1989.

On December 10, the Sunday before his exile, the pastor met once again with his congregation and announced that he had no intention of going quietly. "I will not accept it, so I will be taken from you by force next Friday," he told them.

"They want to do this in secret because they have no right to do it. Please, come next Friday and be witness of what will happen."

His congregation knew the reality of what would happen to their pastor. They had witnessed similar scenes for decades. Students and peasants, pastors and priests—over the years, millions were thrown into prison. Many died there. Between 1945 and 1965, 1,700 of the 9,000 Orthodox priests in Romania were imprisoned. Four out of five Uniate bishops died in prison.[1] Laszlo Tokes's congregation was not about to let that happen to their leader, whom they loved.

That Friday, when the police arrived to arrest Tokes, they met a throng of people who prevented them from making the arrest. Christians from Baptist, Pentecostal, Reformed, and Orthodox backgrounds stood in solidarity with Tokes and one another. As Tokes looked out his window, he saw thousands of candles piercing the darkness.

Soldiers opened fire on the crowd and hundreds died. Yet the demonstrators would not turn back. They entered the town square. By Christmas Day 1989, the revolution had deposed Romania's dictator, Nicolae Ceausescu, and Tokes had been restored to his congregation.

The courage of the Romanian Christian community had sustained a flicker of faith in the country. That flicker became a blaze of the gospel penetrating the darkness of Romania's communism. And in the midst of that movement stood John Maisel, offering hope for a brighter future, but more so, experiencing a change in his own faith, and learning the true meaning of courage.

A DANGEROUS WAIT

In 1987, John was in Romania waiting to secretly meet a Christian leader to take him to a Bible conference he was scheduled to speak at. Men and women were forbidden to gather for Christ's purposes, so he understood the danger he and this leader were in just by meeting. As he stood staring through a dirty store window, he noticed the few cheaply made goods cluttering a table. He thought about how that contrasted starkly with the bright, glimmering shops in the United States filled with new and wondrous merchandise that was available to anyone.

The relentless winds of an intensifying Romanian winter blew against him, and John turned up the collar of his dark, nondescript overcoat. He tugged at his woolen hat, attempting unsuccessfully to pull it farther down over his conspicuously blond hair. So far he had resisted hair dyes and other elaborate disguises, contenting himself with the drab clothing characteristic of the people with whom he sought to blend in. He wanted to do nothing to raise suspicion or give away that he was an American on course to work with believers in Romania to change their country for Christ.

It struck him that he was not nervous as he waited. At least he was not nervous in the way American Christians usually assumed he must be during moments like this as he waited in a secret place in a communist-controlled city.

Certainly there was nothing of the tense fear that had marked some of his worst moments in Vietnam. He carried a heightened awareness, to be sure. It seemed more reminiscent of the eagerness he had always felt waiting for the snap of the ball in his football days. The battle in which he now found himself engaged had at times a game-like quality he found exhilarating, despite the deadly seriousness of the whole business.

He recalled a recent brush with the secret police, which he had thoroughly enjoyed. The memory of the jaunty smile and wave he'd given the wordlessly fuming agent who had followed him into a trolley car a split second before he'd jumped quickly between the closing doors to the pavement still made him chuckle.

He clutched a postcard between the gloved thumb and forefinger of his right hand, a little too tightly perhaps. He tapped it absently against his leg as he resisted the urge to check his watch again. He glanced down the sparsely populated street without moving his head and hoped for the tenth time that he hadn't gotten the time wrong somehow. Even as his mind reviewed every detail, he knew he was in the right spot, at the right time, on the right day.

Perhaps that explained his seemingly irrational calm. He knew he was completely secure in the sovereignty of God, whatever complications or risks arose in the course of his work.

He had always encountered complications and risks in the past. He was always keenly aware that the risk to his Romanian contacts far outweighed any risks he took. At worst, discovery of his activities might mean being detained for a few days or weeks until his government friends in Washington could cut through the red tape and take him

home safely. But such a turn of events might make it difficult for him to travel in the country again, if not downright
impossible—something he wanted to avoid. This country
needed Christ, and if that meant putting himself in danger
to accomplish God's work, then so be it.

Other Americans had been blackballed like that, and
the ministry felt the effects. But the consequences to those
Romanian Christians daring so much to further the work
of the gospel would be far more serious. He remembered
the last unsuccessful rendezvous. After waiting more than
an hour, he gave up and left. Later he learned the man he
was to meet had been arrested just before their scheduled
contact. Police had searched the man's car and discovered
Christian literature. He tried to blink back the thought as it
disturbed his confident state of mind. He breathed in deeply
as he wondered if some evil had befallen the unknown man
he was to meet.

Like a flash, verses from Philippians, the book he was to
teach the believers during the next few days, sprang to his
mind. He felt the Holy Spirit's gentle encouragement as he
mentally recited Philippians 4:6-7: "Do not be anxious about
anything, but in every situation, by prayer and petition, with
thanksgiving, present your requests to God. And the peace
of God, which transcends all understanding, will guard your
hearts and your minds in Christ Jesus."

Immediately he began to pray for the safety of the
stranger he awaited. He prayed for all the others. These
believers were willing to live at great risk for the cause of
Christ in the midst of an atheistic communist society. They

understood the danger they placed themselves in, and yet they willingly chose to identify with their God no matter what the consequences. Some of them might even now be making their way to whatever building had been secured for the clandestine three-day Bible conference.

He had no idea where it even was or how he would get there. It was a strange feeling. He slipped his left hand deep into his coat pocket and closed it over the tiny New Testament tucked among the coded teaching notes. He wanted to "hold fast the word of life" literally as well as figuratively. Then he prayed for his role in the battle. God had quoted Philippians to him, now he wanted to paraphrase it back to God.

"Lord, let me not run in vain nor toil in vain. Your children here are truly lights in the midst of a crooked and perverse generation, and the Enemy would love to use the darkness of communism to keep them from learning more of Your Word this week and sharing it with others. Thank You for the privilege of being here, of striving together for the faith of the gospel. Let me not be alarmed by my opponents. Give me boldness! Let me not be put to shame in anything!"

He wiggled his now semi-numb toes, wishing he had worn an extra pair of socks, when he became aware of a dark, unmoving figure several yards away at the far end of the shop window. The man seemed to have come out of nowhere and stood quietly staring at the merchandise. John's heart leapt.

There it was, dangling from the thumb and forefinger in his left hand—a postcard. John suppressed a relieved smile. The dark man lifted his head slightly, met his eyes for a fraction of a second, and turned and walked away from him. John breathed a silent prayer of thanks and forced himself to count to ten before following the stranger.

A SECRET MEETING

John was careful to maintain a fair distance between himself and the figure ahead of him. He knew better than to look over his shoulder, but he made a few sideways glances as he rounded various corners during their odd parade. It confirmed what he already assumed: another of their own, a stranger like the first, was keeping pace with John at a safe distance to ensure that he had not been followed to the site of the rendezvous.

So far so good, John thought.

One by one, the three men made their way among the look-alike pedestrians leaning doggedly into the wind. There was a sameness to these people that John found almost eerie—everyone's heads bent, all eyes downcast. They were all bundled in shabby clothing as cheerless as their expressions.

John couldn't help but wonder, *What sorts of things go through their minds as they shuffle through the blackened slush? Does anyone ever get "used to" living under the heel of oppression? Do their hearts long for the light the way these dreary streets long for sunshine and color? What are the chances that these passing souls will ever hear the Good News about the Light of the world?*

Though he couldn't answer his ponderings, he did know one thing for certain: he was there to increase their odds of seeing that Light.

As they marched on, the gathering dusk served as his only gauge of the passing time. They had been walking through unfamiliar areas of the city for some time. John's heart filled with sadness. No matter where they were, the scene was the same: sad people and bleak, dilapidated buildings. As he glanced at the building, with a wry smile tugging at the corner of his mouth, John recalled one of his first journeys behind the Iron Curtain. A man there had asked him to guess the age of a certain typically run-down apartment building. It had every appearance of being fifteen or twenty years old, but his companion had laughed at the estimate. Incredulously, the building was only two years old.

He rounded yet another corner onto yet another gray side street and paused abruptly. The stranger he followed stood facing him near the end of the short block, motioning urgently for John to hurry as a small battered car pulled up to the curb at the far corner. John broke into a sprint, reaching the vehicle only moments after his companion had opened the back door.

John dove in, followed by the stranger he had followed. As the man slammed the car door, the driver put the ancient, grinding gears into drive and pulled away. They passed the unknown friend who had ensured John's safety. He gave an almost imperceptible glance and nodded toward the car as he rounded the corner and continued walking.

John fell back against the seat with a now wide and open grin. Taking a deep breath, he turned to face his nameless brother. The man returned his grin with a joyous light in his eyes and added a deep, low laugh. It was infectious, and John found himself laughing back and clasping the man's hand as if he were an old friend. It was the only way they could communicate, since John couldn't speak the man's language, but it was enough.

Darkness descended as the rattling automobile wound through endlessly twisting streets and finally pulled clear of the city altogether. Long after it was too dark to see within the car, the men continued periodically to grin at each other. Their heartfelt connection warmed John as the vehicle's capricious heater could not. The luminous dial of his watch told him they had been bouncing along the rough country roads for close to an hour. Finally, they turned onto an unpaved path even darker than the road they were leaving. Slowing to a crawl, the driver extinguished the fitful light cast by the dirty headlights.

John strained to make out his surroundings, but the clouds obscured even the moon's faint gleam. As the car came to a halt, he wondered how the driver could possibly navigate in such blackness. The driver flashed his light three times. Each time John saw that they had paused at a large wooden gate, apparently the entrance to a sort of barnyard.

The gate swung slowly open, and the darkened car crept into the yard. A house, quite sizeable by Romanian standards, loomed ahead. Except for a squawking, startled chicken, all was silent as they coasted down a slight incline past the outhouse and an apparently deserted pigsty and rolled to a stop. Wordlessly everyone alighted from the car as a shadowy figure opened the house's front door.

John followed his companion inside the house. Blankets covered the windows of the unlit dwelling, and the resulting blackness combined with the complete silence made John feel as if he were moving in a dream. Instinctively he stretched out his hand to brush the coat of the brother ahead of him and was instantly reminded of night marches in Vietnam. They shuffled forward hugging the wall and trying not to trip over anything as they trekked deep into the interior of the house. At last they passed through a doorway and stopped. He sensed more than heard the slight rustlings and steady breathing filling the space. Suddenly light flooded the room, causing John to squint even as tears unexpectedly filled his eyes.

More than thirty Christians filled the room, some in chairs, more on the floor, beaming, eager Christians with upturned faces full of gratitude. John wondered how they had all come to be there. Many had probably walked long distances. He knew it was not unusual for some individuals to travel more than eight hundred miles just to bask in the light of God's Word. Their faces were radiant with joy and thanksgiving, and John swallowed hard in an unsuccessful attempt to clear the lump in his throat. These courageous Romanian Christians had risked it all, literally, to follow Jesus. And though John had traveled to minister to them, they infused within him a desire to live courageously in his free society where God had placed him.

He opened his mouth to greet them but closed it again, unable to break the silence. Scriptures echoed in his heart more resoundingly than any human speech: "That you may declare the praises of Him who called you out of darkness into his wonderful light" (1 Peter 2:9). These thirty courageous Christians were emblematic of the courageous Christians throughout Romania. They had endured more than forty years of communistic oppression.

John now knew why he had gone to Romania. God wanted to teach him the meaning of courage—courage that involved brave choices and lifestyles. Not theoretical stories but living the bold and daring reality of following Jesus, no matter what.

CHAPTER 8

THE COURAGE TO GO PUBLIC

John returned to the United States with his strong lessons in courage, after seeing what the people in oppressed societies risked to worship God. He felt great concern over the state of Christianity in his homeland. Particularly, he saw how comfortable the church had become.

He grew concerned over the silence of the American church, or what he refers to as the "epidemic of silence," believing this issue is the consequence of not living or leading with courage. As more and more evil has begun to penetrate the country, and clear morals and values have been altered, John has watched with dismay and frustration as the church has done little to fight against it.

John isn't alone in his concern. The impact of the current trends is devastating. In his essay *The Great Opportunity,* Josh Crossman outlined the current trajectory of American Christianity. Crossman, the CEO and founding board member of his family foundation Pinetops, spent a great deal of time as a leader in the social-sector practice working with large philanthropies, governments, and social ventures to solve tough problems in society.

In his report Crossman wrote, "If trends continue the American church will lose 1 million young people per year until the year 2050. That represents a loss of 35 million young people from the church between 2015 and 2050. If trends continue, we will see the closing of 176,000 churches in America by 2050."[1] Crossman and John Maisel share the same observation: that a weakened witness to our culture will continue the rapid decline of the US church.

The impact of this on American culture and the role of the American church in world missions would be catastrophic. With the stakes so extraordinarily high, John's reflections on not playing it safe are more prescient than ever. What does John believe is the answer? The alternative is to go public with our witness for Jesus Christ. Here are John's thoughts in his own words.

PLAYING IT SAFE IS NOT AN OPTION

Before you and I will ever be willing to take the risk necessary in our culture that comes from the *Yes, Lord, no matter what* mentality, we must have a firm belief. That belief is about the truth of God's way—that what God desires for us will always result for our highest good.

The reason we play it safe and don't rock the boat of culture is because we don't truly believe that pain, rejection, career losses, failure, and abandonment will really work for our highest good. We are afraid that we might lose something we think is necessary for us to be really happy. No one seeks painful reactions, and it is certainly not biblical to seek suffering for the sake of suffering. We must be aware that we will encounter trouble and difficulty as we follow Christ—and we must be convinced that it is okay.

We will never step out of our comfort zones or feel less fearful or adequate unless we are convinced that God's way, no matter what, will always result in our good. The walk of faith is, for the most part, learning to be content when mystery is all around us related to what God is doing, because we trust His heart and sovereign purposes to accomplish His good will.

I believe the greatest limitation of the conquering march of Jesus Christ today is not:

- Secularism
- Materialism
- Commercialism
- Atheism
- Islam

The greatest limitation is Christians who know they have their seat in heaven, who play it safe and don't want to take seriously the radical claims of Jesus Christ upon our lives.

What do you really believe?

- I am an alien on earth.
- My true citizenship is in heaven.
- Christ's love is better than life.

- I possess the power to be His witness.
- He has sent me on a mission.

Do you really believe that? If you do, then you can say:

- All I have is His—my present day and my future career.
- My life is to focus on bringing people to Him in accordance to my giftedness.
- Christ's love will drive me to say, "Yes, Lord, no matter what."
- My unquenchable thirst will be to serve Him and carry out His purpose "no matter what."

The heart of Georgy Slesarev is what I desperately desire for my life. He is one of my heroes and a twentieth-century model for what I am trying to say about each of our callings to follow passionately the "Jesus of the Scriptures." He was a Russian Christian who lived before our time, and he had the heart to be God's man where he lived and God's witness in a dangerous culture.

For nine years Georgy Slesarev was the lead violinist for the Bolshoi Theater orchestra in Moscow. He was a gifted musician and a committed Christian. Late on the night of January 21, 1935, the secret police arrested him and charged him with crimes against the state. He was accused of actively witnessing to others about his faith in Jesus. His sentence was five years of hard labor at the camp of Temir-Tau in Kazakhstan, near the Siberian border. After he had served almost three years, his wife and daughter were allowed to travel to visit him for their one and only time.

The day before Slesarev was to see his precious family, the prison warden offered him an incredible opportunity. He could return home with his wife and daughter the next day and assume his job in the orchestra. The only stipulation was that he promise never to witness of his faith in Christ or associate with Christians again. This he could not do.

He was allowed a brief visit with his wife and daughter the next day, but he could not bring himself to tell them of the offer his captors had made. Soon after, he was transferred to a work group doing hard manual labor. His hands that had once played the violin so masterfully were broken and swollen and would never make music again.

In March 1938, Slesarev was convicted of witnessing to fellow inmates about his faith in Jesus. He was sentenced to be executed by firing squad. Shortly before his death, Slesarev confided in a Christian friend in the camp, "My dear brother, don't grieve. Christ has become so close to me. He is closer than He has ever been. My flesh is weak, my body is tired, but this is just a temporary moment in the time of eternity that is soon to open up to me. They have stopped me from playing the violin, but my dear, dear friend, you know, you understand, that they cannot stop the music that plays inside my heart."[2]

Georgy Slesarev could have lived his life doing what he loved and being "politically correct" as a secret Christian on the job, but he didn't. How about the excuse that many of us use in trying to play it safe when we say, "Well, I'm not trained or educated properly"?

We act as though all the public things about Jesus need to be communicated by the professionals who have gone to seminary. Since I have never gone to seminary other than "street seminary" in the marketplace of life, I take much encouragement from the lives of Peter and John. In the Bible, they were called, "unschooled, ordinary men" (Acts 4:13). When the people there "saw the courage of Peter and John and realized that they were unschooled, ordinary men, they were astonished and they took note that these men had been with Jesus."

Peter and John were breaking down walls in the religious thinking to the Jewish population and religious leaders of that day. They could have chosen not to go public because they had a good excuse according to today's thinking. They were uneducated and untrained men.

Peter and John communicated the fact that Jesus was the answer to all they would need in the future. When men and women begin to think and act that way, it causes social tension. Because of the controversies they were addressing, many of the religious leaders thought Peter and John needed to be silent. These religious leaders had brought them in and told them to "back off" and not to "speak or teach at all in the name of Jesus."

I believe that God is still looking for men and women who will stand gripped in His grace. As best as we know how, we must have the courage to identify with Jesus Christ in all situations. These "unschooled, ordinary men" give us a clear picture of what "courageous choices" look like.

How will Peter and John react? What do they really believe about Jesus? They are at a crossroads. Do we really believe and value God's way more than any culture's logical thinking?

If I act contrary to what the religious society of my day says, what will I lose or what will I gain that affects my happiness? Peter and John acted with courage because they really believed that God's way, God's truth, and God's care would lead and guide them into the experience of life that was best for them. So they responded in Acts 4:19-20: "Which is right in God's eyes: to listen to you, or to him? You be the judges! As for us, we cannot help speaking about what we have seen and heard."

In this situation they were released unharmed. Later in life, where they applied the same belief to their making God's way more than man's way, Peter would get crucified upside down and John would be exiled to Patmos by himself. Why did God use them? Because they didn't care about themselves, only about whether or not God was pleased.

In Acts 5:40 we read that they got flogged and ordered not to speak in the name of Jesus and then released. What was their attitude?

"The apostles left the Sanhedrin, rejoicing because they had been counted worthy of suffering disgrace for the Name. Day after day, in the temple courts and from house to house, they never stopped teaching and proclaiming the good news that Jesus is the Messiah" (Acts 5:41-42).

We must learn to apply the same principles when we are in situations that require us to compromise Jesus by remaining silent about Him. Courage will only act if we really believe that God's way and God's glory are always the best for us and our families. Action always flows from what we believe. Action determines what we truly value, and what we value will determine what we do.

All they asked Peter and John to do was not to go public with Jesus. But because of this core value that God's way and God's glory are always what is best, no matter what happened in the short run they acted with courage. Their choices were based on a higher value that honoring Christ is of greater value than the comfortable life. Because they really believed that to be true, they acted with courage, willing to risk loss and injury for the hope of gaining God the glory due His name.

You and I must continually ask ourselves, "What do I really believe?" For *only* what we do tells us what we *really* believe. Courage to act is not natural but supernatural when it comes to the ways of God, and we as "the bride of Christ" need to pray for this type of holy boldness, which is always mixed with meekness.

An insight that we don't want to miss in this Acts 4 passage is how they prayed. I am a firm believer that we can pray about anything and everything. Philippians 4 tells us to "make our requests known to God"—any request. I do feel that too much of our prayer life is about ourselves and our safety, our comfort, our protection, and our success.

Peter didn't pray that way. He prayed that they would be given boldness to speak the name of Jesus (see Acts 4:29). He asked for courage, because the people around him who disagreed with him were making threats that if he went public, he could expect the worst. Peter was not driven by what the outcome would be. Was he scared? Probably. That is why he asked for the courage he needed to honor and glorify God.

The same situation happened to Paul in 1 Corinthians 2, when he had an opportunity to speak out about Christ. He was "fearful and scared" about what was going to happen. The Spirit infused courage to pull the trigger that released the power of God in that situation. His value was that "for I determined to know nothing among you except Jesus Christ, and Him crucified" (1 Corinthians 2:2, NASB).

This is what Paul said he really believed, but would he go public with his faith even though his feelings were telling him rejection, trouble, and difficulty awaited him? He was scared as he made clear when he wrote, "I was with you in weakness and in fear and in much trembling" (1 Corinthians 2:3, NASB).

I would imagine that where the combination of weakness and fear come together, much trembling takes place. Because he stepped out with courage, God began to move. His message, he said, was "in demonstration of the Spirit and of power" (1 Corinthians 2:4, NASB), and people were set free from darkness through Christ. A church was given birth as he acted on what he believed rather than what he feared.

What if Paul had followed his fear and valued his "self-protection" and the safety of not being rejected more than acting with courage? What would have happened? God would have worked another way to reach the Corinthians, but Paul would have never gotten to see what God would have done. That, my friend, is the greatest consequence of not living with courage in our politically, culturally, and religiously correct society.

If we live to ourselves, for ourselves, and through ourselves, we never get to see what God could have done through us if we would just say yes to Him no matter what. No action, no courage, no movement of God's presence, power, or plan will take place apart from our courage.

Mark Twain reportedly once said that "courage is resistance to fear, mastery of fear, not absence of fear." Choosing to act, even when afraid, is a good understanding of the virtues of courage, which is the need of my own heart as I walk through life. Paul is a great model of valuing God's values more than what my fear tells me I will lose if I do this or how I will upset my society standards.

Paul was driven by this paradigm for all of his life. He stated in Philippians 1:19-20 (NASB):

> I know that this will turn out for my deliverance
> through your prayers and the provision of the Spirit
> of Jesus Christ, according to my earnest expectation
> and hope, that I will not be put to shame in anything,
> but that with all boldness [courage], Christ will even
> now, as always, be exalted in my body.

Then he added this little but profound statement, "Whether by life or by death."

In other words, how the situation worked out was not his concern—his driving passion was: "Have I done that which magnifies, honors, and glorifies Jesus Christ no matter what the outcome?"

Granted that most if not all of what God may ask of the

Christians in America will not result in death. But there are definitely places in the world where that statement is factual.

There is a basis for addressing this in our culture if we are to live courageously in our walk with Christ. I believe each of us who has said yes to Jesus in our lives, desires to honor Him with our lives. Yes, there is much failure in the body of Christ in living out the reality of our faith, but I believe there is great potential.

God has ordained the possibility to live courageously. I believe Christians want to live this way. We need to come to grips with our convictions and make some faith decisions that will free us to be all God intended us to be.

In America, we can't add, "whether by life or by death," as our faith rarely will cost us our lives. We need to face the reality of what cost may be involved. In America with all our freedom, we can say, "Yes, Lord, no matter what—whether I have success or experience failure, whether I get the job or lose the job, whether good things happen to me or bad experiences develop." Scripture gives us a great understanding of this in Paul's experience and the experience of many other saints in the Bible.

Let's take Paul and his commitment to go up to Jerusalem, which we begin to see unfold in the book of Acts. Our first insight comes in Acts 20:22-23 when he talked about going Jerusalem: "Now, behold, bound in spirit, I am on my way to Jerusalem, not knowing what will happen to me there, except that the Holy Spirit solemnly testifies to me in every city, saying that bonds and afflictions await me" (NASB).

Notice he said, "I am bound in spirit." I take that to mean

God was leading and telling him He wanted him in Jerusalem, but God informed him that very tough, difficult, and painful circumstances would await him when he arrived there. Later, other brothers and sisters asked him not to go up to the city because they knew the trouble that was awaiting him.

But Paul answered, "What are you doing, weeping and breaking my heart? For I am ready not only to be bound, but even to die at Jerusalem for the name of the Lord Jesus" (Acts 21:13, NASB).

What was his frame of reference for this situation? It was the same as in Philippians 1:19-20 when he spoke about God's purposes and Christ being called attention to. Here in Acts 20:24, he said the same thing in a different way: "I do not consider my life of any account as dear to myself, in order that I may finish my course, and the ministry which I received from the Lord Jesus to testify solemnly of the gospel of the grace of God" (NASB).

Paul's thinking—and our thinking—is to be coura-geously acted upon, disregarding the results or outcome. The only result that Paul was assured of was that if he obeyed, God would receive honor and Christ's name would become famous, no matter how it turned out, knowing that he could trust God to work it out for His purpose and glory. The reason Paul was so radical was his belief that if God was honored and glorified in a situation, then this was for his highest good.

May we take that important lesson and apply it to our own lives and ministry.

PART THREE

JOHN'S LEGACY

CHAPTER 9

A MENTOR'S MENTOR

One of the most amazing gifts John has is his ability to make quick friends. He makes people feel valued, a skill that has helped him in his leadership and in his mission to grow disciples of Jesus.

The men quoted in this chapter are all serious professional marketplace leaders. They are leaders in their own right. And yet John has had a profound impact on them. As you read their stories, which reflect John's character traits, consider how God may be calling you to emulate John's actions.

LIVE AND BREATHE THE GOSPEL

Butch McCaslin, partner at McCaslin, Barrow, and Henderson

Forty years ago, John and I served on the board of Career Impact Ministry, an organization that focused on the belief that every marketplace leader was a minister. We connected immediately and have retained a close, personal relationship.

So much so, that when John founded East-West Ministries, I served as a founding board member and stayed on the board for twenty-three years. During that time, I have been on numerous mission trips to India, Russia, and Cuba with John. I consider him both a mentor and one of my very best friends.

Watching his life has impacted my life and who I strive to be. He is totally, completely, unequivocally sold out to Jesus Christ. More than once he has told me, "Butch, Jesus Christ is as real to me as you are." The first time he said that, well, that took me back, and I have had to think about it over time. But he doesn't just say the words; he means them. Over these forty years of knowing him, I've watched the reality of his relationship with Jesus Christ. And what he says is true.

He is so consumed with his relationship with Jesus and his involvement in expanding the Kingdom that he can't think, talk, or spend any time other than focusing on Jesus. When you are around him, you can't deny it. Day in, day out. Particularly you see it in his approach to Scripture. He is addicted to the Bible. He must have it with him and open all the time. He studies it. He has an uncommon appetite, a unique insight into the Scriptures. He teaches it masterfully. The Bible is his roadmap.

He doesn't just read the Scriptures, he applies them. I most profoundly saw that through his work with East-West. He says three things are the founding, basic principles for East-West Ministries: (1) pursue Jesus; (2) pursue Jesus; (3) pursue Jesus. That is all, and it has been all since East-West's formation in 1993.

We can easily see the fruits of that mentality: East-West

has gone from a local ministry to expanding internationally, starting in Russia and then spreading globally. Because of Christ's work through East-West, tens of millions of people have professed faith in Jesus Christ.

John cannot cross paths with anyone—whether it is at a restaurant, on the street, in the halls of an office, or in the marketplace—without telling them about the unmerited grace of Jesus Christ and the opportunity to know him personally.

If you were somehow able to ask the New Testament believers who followed Paul around, "What was his greatest impact?" they would undoubtedly say, "I've watched Christ's reality through him. He was a man of resolve and determination, and that made him immensely effective for the cause of Christ." Undeniably that's the way I feel about John. To me, he's a modern-day Paul.

Every year at Thanksgiving, our family shares what they are most thankful for. Every year I say the same thing: I'm thankful for my friendship with John Maisel.

John challenged me for forty years to be the man God wants me to be. He has never let up. I've watched how he has approached his life, so I've got no excuse. I know what it looks like to be totally immersed in the reality of serving the risen Savior. I've seen it because I've seen John.

INTRODUCE JESUS TO EVERYONE

Chuck Anderson, partner at Bandera Ventures
Commercial Real Estate

Without John I wouldn't know who Jesus is. Literally. John introduced me to Jesus when I attended a Bible study with a small group of friends. He changed the course of my life and eternity, so I'm forever grateful.

I'm not the only one who has John to thank for that introduction. John shares the gospel with everyone he meets. Every time I am with John, he shares the gospel with somebody and encourages me to share the gospel with somebody. The last time I was with him, we were at a restaurant and I watched him share the gospel with our server. His passion and excitement are infectious.

That's John's greatest legacy: he has taught a lot of guys how to share Christ with people. Those conversations and encounters have had a huge influence on me because I try to emulate what he does. He tells me, "Look, Chuck, if all else fails, talk about Jesus."

VALUE COMMUNITY

Kenneth Aboussie, managing partner, Stonelake Capital Partners

Several years ago, John asked for football tickets for him and his grandson to the Oklahoma–Texas game. We were at the Cotton Bowl in Dallas. John and his grandson sat in front of us. At one point I looked down at John and had to smile. He had four *Is Jesus God?* booklets stuffed into his back pocket. Even surrounded by 110,000 screaming Texas and Oklahoma fans at a sport that John loves, he still thinks he is on a mission trip at the state fair of Texas.

John is all about building God's Kingdom. But he isn't interested in just bringing in new people; he's interested in growing disciples. That's what he has done for me. John taught me the importance of getting serious about my faith in Christ and living for the Lord. He would often quote Hebrews 10:23-25 to me: "Let us hold unswervingly to the hope we profess, for he who promised is faithful. And let us consider how we may spur one another on toward love and good deeds, not giving up meeting together."

For the past five years John has led a Bible study every Thursday at lunch in our office's conference room. The men who attend are newly married or engaged, or with young families. John has gotten to know these thirty guys, loving on them and encouraging them as they walk through challenges; he has no draw or reason other than his commitment to disciple men.

What is even more impressive is that these men are not CEOs of companies. John could just meet with CEOs, but he has chosen to meet with and pour into younger guys too. These young businessmen have received immense wise counsel from John. They have been able to understand the Word of God better through his teaching and been encouraged by men getting together.

LOVE LIKE JESUS

Jeff Swope, founder, Champion Partners

Other than my wife, I've never had anybody love on me like John Maisel. I compare it to how Jesus loved on His disciples. That is just the way you feel when you are with John. He projects love toward you the way Jesus would project love toward you.

I met John twelve years ago and we had lunch. I felt that love then. He was somebody who *knew* Jesus but also admitted his brokenness, admitted his difficulties, but also knew there was only one way through them—Jesus. That was my first experience with John, and I wanted to get together more often!

We have been to Asia together. We have been to Latin America together, and we've spent countless experiences together. It's always the same: he loves me like Jesus loves me. Now I am one of the executors of his estate. I see his desire to honor Jesus in his estate-planning work. It is intoxicating to see someone live with such a zeal to honor God in every detail of his life even to the end.

My favorite memory of John was during an East-West mission trip to Asia. Five of us were standing in a circle waiting to pray. One morning I took the lead and began praying, "Bless us for the day. Thank You for the opportunities of this trip to share the gospel. You know how much we love You."

Suddenly, John said, "Butch, will you start?"

We all broke out laughing because that was John. He was already praying in another dimension. He then realized he needed to get back to the group and be part of our prayer. He was so focused on his praying that he had not heard me praying. He is so focused and desirous of his relationship with Jesus Christ, it eclipses everything else happening around him. And even though we all laughed, I never took offense, because I knew what was happening, and I knew that he meant nothing but a richness of love toward all of us—something that poured out of him because of his deep relationship with Christ.

I almost tear up when I say it: I think John's greatest

legacy is that he is probably the closest on earth to a person who is most like Jesus. To love like that is an amazing legacy.

PROVIDE AN ANCHOR OF GRACE

Pryor Blackwell, partner, Bandera Ventures
Commercial Real Estate

As a child I thought God was something to be feared, so I did. As an adult when I met John, it changed all that for me. The concept of grace and mercy completely diminished the fear I felt, and his certainty around God's grace and undeserved favor became an anchor for me—something I would desperately need.

In 2008 my wife and I lost a son tragically and unexpectedly. I struggled with grief and depression as I was trying to come to terms with his death and sort out why something this terrible could happen.

John was trying to be reassuring, which he is so good at doing. I would get notes and calls from him from time to time. They always referenced a Bible verse. One morning, while I was having breakfast with him, I lost my cool with him over the fact that he kept offering Bible verses to reassure me. I harshly lashed out at John.

John sat quietly for a minute, then he asked me a question that changed everything: "If I were not sitting here and your son was here for only five minutes, what would he say to you?"

I began to weep uncontrollably. All of a sudden, I connected with my son, with that grief, and with God. I connected with the reassurance that God would redeem what He allowed going forward.

BLESS OTHERS

Jody Thornton, president, HFF Real Estate

I grew up in Fort Worth and was deeply influenced by Young Life. Young Life ministries had a strong emphasis on sharing the gospel. Until I met John, I had never seen anyone who had such a spirit for evangelism everywhere he went. John loved on me just as he has loved on everyone. His capacity to love others is so extraordinary.

Growing up I never thought I would go on mission trips and evangelize the way John has taught me. Yet I went on my first mission trip to Latin America in 2005. It was the first time I can remember sharing my faith with other people cross-culturally.

My favorite memory of John is when I saw Reverend Criswell from First Baptist Church in Dallas meet him. In his prime Reverend Criswell was one of the most influential pastors in America at one of the largest churches in Dallas. By the time he and John were introduced to each other, Reverend Criswell was in decline and confined to a wheelchair.

When they met, John knelt in front of Reverend Criswell's wheelchair to speak to him face-to-face. Reverend Criswell grabbed John by the face and said, "You're a good boy, Maisel." Every time I remember that I choke up. It was a bit like seeing the mantle of leadership transfer from one legend to another.

BE BOLD AND OBEDIENT

Tom Leiser, partner, Bandera Ventures Commercial Real Estate

I can characterize the impact of John in two words: *boldness* and *obedience*. When you think about Jesus' final words on earth, "Go and make disciples of all nations," John has obeyed that command with great obedience.

I know because I've seen it firsthand. I took my first short-term mission trip with John. I learned how important it was to share the gospel boldly. I learned how important it was to be comfortable sharing the gospel in a variety of circumstances. And I learned that by watching John.

When we were on a trip together to Kazakhstan, we encountered a problem with the plane. We were broken down on the tarmac in Baku, Azerbaijan. The cabin of plane was sweltering in the heat; it was more than one hundred degrees. A young Muslim man sitting across from me took off his shirt, which was the first time I'd flown with someone shirtless.

All I could think about was how uncomfortable I was in the heat and how I had to stare at a shirtless man. John had other things on his mind, however. I watched as he pulled out his gospel tract and began sharing the Bible with some other young Muslim women and men. It hit me that perhaps God was calling me to do that too. John has always modeled what he has asked others to do.

As I have thought about John's legacy, I'm reminded of one of my favorite books by Randy Alcorn, *Heaven*. Randy speculates that part of the way we are going to spend eternity is by being greeted by all the people we have directly or indirectly affected for Christ. Eternity might need overtime for all the people whom John has impacted through his ministry. Just because he was bold in his obedience.

REMEMBER OUR RESPONSIBILITY

Pryor Blackwell, partner, Bandera Ventures
Commercial Real Estate

John has been a mentor to me in a number of ways, one of them I spoke to on a previous page about providing an anchor of grace. But there's another way I value his mentorship. Before I met John, I was one of those people who viewed their faith mainly as a responsibility to go to church and attend Bible study. It's a neat, safe, tidy spiritual journey. But John is a guerilla Christian. He goes where no one wants to go. He goes where he's unwelcome but badly needed. He goes regardless of the risk to him. He thinks it is that important.

Once while I was visiting with him, we were talking about the importance of evangelism. He suggested that there is a line at a door and the door leads to the gates of hell. Every day people all over the world stand in that line, open that door, and walk through it because no one took the time to share the gospel with them.

John said, "It is our responsibility to stand at that door and stop them. We can't keep them from going through it, but we have a responsibility to share our faith with them and to share the gospel of Jesus Christ, because if we let them go through that door, in a way we were complicit in that experience for them. Eternity is a long time. If we don't share the gospel just because we are uncomfortable or someone might criticize us, then we need to remember our responsibility."

STEP INTO YOUR OWN SHOES

Kurt Nelson, president & CEO, East-West Ministries

Following John Maisel as a leader was probably the most daunting task I ever stepped into. I remember eight years ago when I became president and CEO of East-West. Just thinking about how big his shoes are and the impossibility of my trying to fill them felt formidable. Finally, as I continued to worry over it, the Lord said to me, *You don't have to fill his shoes. You have to fill your own shoes.*

John has been a phenomenal advocate, a tremendous encouragement. I have found a great model in following John as John follows Jesus. John has walked with me for the last eight years. He has stood and supported me, encouraged me, and championed me. He has always been willing to speak into my life and heart.

It has never been about me being John. It has been about me being the best Kurt Nelson I can be. John and I have met offsite every month for the last eight years in order to keep short accounts with each other. It has been the greatest privilege of my life not only to work for John for fifteen years, but then to follow John for the last eight years. Because of his humility, his gentleness, and his own passion to see Christ formed in and through me, he has made me a better leader.

IT IS 99 PERCENT SHOWING UP AND 1 PERCENT YOU

Mark Gibson, CEO, HFF Real Estate

On one of our mission trips to Latin America, John was not allowed into the country we were visiting. As we left him and continued on, he told our group, "Remember it is 99 percent showing up and 1 percent you." That turned out to be exactly the case. We went to houses with twenty or so people in them. We spoke the prepared comments we had, which were very simple and very short. And the Holy Spirit used that. The people's response was undeniable and overwhelming as we watched over and over nearly all of them accept the gospel. It was a lesson on presence.

John became a hugely important mentor in my life. One time I was thinking of becoming a vocational ministry leader. John helped me to understand that any mission field is as important to God as any other. He challenged me to consider my work as a marketplace leader as the most important mission field.

John is going to have a huge host waiting for him in heaven. It doesn't matter with John whether you are with him, talking to him on the phone, or at an event. He understands the importance of presence. He shows up and God does His work through John.

John is all in all the time.

CHAPTER 10

LOOKING TOWARD THE FUTURE

On March 2, 2018, the world watched the funeral of Billy Graham. Looking at the audience gathered that day, my wife, Marya, and I were filled with gratitude as we saw giants of the faith—Henry Blackaby, Rick Warren, and so many others—who have led so faithfully for so long.

And yet we recognized a deep sadness: not only was Billy Graham gone, but most of the spiritual leaders in attendance that day would also be gone within a decade or two at best. In 2018 alone, we saw the passing of Billy Graham, Bob Buford, and Eugene Peterson. Their presence leaves a noticeable and gaping hole and makes us wonder, *What will the next generation look like?* We were seeing the changing of the guard, a passing generation, in American Christian leadership.

We also come to the close of this book recognizing that John Maisel is counted among that group of passing giants. Although his life may leave us, his legacy will not. His story will continue to be told, to strengthen and encourage countless believers as he passes the mantle of godly leadership to others. And so, in the spirit of mentorship and godly counsel, I include John's words to motivate us to heed the apostle Paul's admonition in Galatians 6:9 to "not become weary in doing good." The following is a message he gave on December 14, 2018, at an East-West luncheon.

PLAYING YOUR "BIT" PART

During World War II, on June 6, 1944, the Allies landed at Normandy, France, to wage a war. It was a real war. Simple orders were given—really simple orders. One hundred and fifty thousand men landed on the beaches of Normandy with the orders to "invade Europe and move to Berlin." All those soldiers were different people, different sizes, different nationalities, different financial situations, different giftedness, different responsibilities, different aspects. But together they were called to invade Europe and move toward Berlin.

There's a raging war taking place for the hearts and minds of people today. It's called a cosmic conflict, and it's happening all around us. And it's real warfare. The battle's been won. But in Ephesians 6:12, Paul reminds us that we fight not against flesh and blood, but against powers, principalities, and kingdoms of darkness. You and I are part of an all-out frontal assault on the kingdom of darkness, which is taking people and cutting their lives off from the living God, from the abundant life and the forgiveness of sin, from receiving the free gift of eternal life.

Every person who is a follower of Christ has a part in

this fight. You cannot sit on the sidelines if the King of Glory has taken up residence within your life. It's a disobedience of orders. Every one of us has a part, that's the beauty of the body of Christ.

Paul wrote in Colossians, "I do my share on behalf of his body, which is the church" (1:24, NASB). Around the East-West office we call it having a "bit part." I've got a "bit part"; you've got a "bit part." You play your "bit part," I play my "bit part," and together we play our "bit parts," and Jesus steps in and He plays His great and magnificent part.

You see, you've got to share in this work. You're part of this equation. The reason you're here on earth today is because you're part of the mission. No matter what you do, no matter what your career, your marital or family status, or your economic status, if you've been captured by Christ, you're on mission.

Matthew shows us a beautiful picture of what this looks like. In Matthew 14, we read that Jesus has been out speaking all day to a crowd of five thousand men, not counting all the women and children, so probably the crowd was about ten thousand people. Toward the end of the day, the disciples start to become anxious, because the people haven't eaten. They approach Jesus and say, "Look, these people have been here all day, they've been listening all day, and they haven't had anything to eat *all day*. We've got to send them away or we might have a riot on our hands."

Jesus, in classic God-Man form, says, "You feed them."

Ten thousand people and Jesus wants the disciples to feed them all! He wants them to do their bit part in becoming the solution. So he asks them what they have. They answer they have five loaves of bread and two fish.

"Break it up," he tells them, "and start feeding the people."

The disciples know if they do that, they will have a riot on their hands for sure. But Peter and maybe some of the others think, *You know, I better do what He says. He's told us to do things like this before, and He's got a way of connecting the dots.* So they divide the food among the twelve of them and they spread out, giving away what they have.

All of a sudden, the food isn't disappearing, it's multiplying.

"Hey, are you guys seeing what I'm seeing?" a disciple says.

"Yeah, it seems like the more we give away, the more it seems to multiply and the more that I have," another says.

After they feed the entire crowd, they still have plenty of food left over.

There's an incredible lesson here. Most of us can feel threatened with a "bit part" God has called us to. But we need to understand that when God asks us to do something, God intends to get involved in the process. And all He asks you to do is what you can do—and then factor in Jesus for the impossible.

THE BATTLE BEGINS WITH YOU

Jesus is not looking for perfect people. I tell people the biggest fight I have every day is not out "there" in the world; it's within my own heart. Can you relate?

We've got a relentless enemy who has lost us, and we've

become sons and daughters of a great Savior. But our enemy wants to do everything he can to get us off mission and away from what God has called us to do. It's a simple mission: Go into the world and preach the gospel. Go and make disciples of all nations. In other words, it seems to me there's an aspect of our Christian experience that is to be verbal.

A lot of people will say, "My Christian life is personal." They're right, it is personal, and it better be personal. But it was never intended to be private. It was intended to go public.

I think one of the things Jesus is trying to teach imperfect people like us is that we need to forget the past. We all have things we're ashamed of. Even the apostle Paul had a pretty bad past with Christians. He approved of Christians being stoned to death, he approved of Christians being locked up. But he was radically changed with his encounter with the living Christ. And he said the thing that we need to embrace: "I've learned to forget that which is behind, and to press toward the make of the high calling of Christ Jesus."

Forget the past. Acknowledge and confess your sins; put them under the blood of Christ, because they've been paid for.

The Enemy comes with condemnation and tries to take us down. But Jesus says, "My brother, My sister, there is no condemnation. I paid the debt in full." So whatever's in the past, sin-wise, you can be sure that if you're struggling with a *Woe is me* mentality, it's coming from the Enemy.

You know the second thing that's in the past? And probably most of us struggle with this one more—it's our successes. We must be very careful about embracing our successes.

Whatever successes you have, however God has used

you, however you're hoping and praying to God to continue to use you, you know what you do with your successes? You lay them at the feet of Jesus, and you don't touch them. You put them behind you and you forget them.

Everything in the past—the good, the bad, and the ugly—has simply been to prepare you for what God wishes to do in and through you in the future. Your successes, your sins.

There's a very important truth to give you the freedom that the grace of God offers, and that's the fact that whatever God has taken you through, He wishes to use it for His glory and for His name's sake once it's laid at His feet. So if you're struggling with your failures, or if you're struggling with your successes, that's your field of mission—to lay them down and then to help others lay theirs down as well, because you can identify with the struggle.

I think it's easy for Christians to become content with our spiritual condition. I've known a number of people, good Christians, who worked hard for the Kingdom until they were about fifty or sixty and then they stopped pushing forward, as though they thought, *I've done my part; I think it's time to coast. I'm going to enjoy myself and let the younger ones do the hard work now.*

Don't become one of those people. Don't become content with your spiritual condition. Know wherever you are in your walk, the best is yet to be.

THIS WORLD NEEDS COURAGEOUS HOPE

The church is the hope of the world, so we must come out of hiding and become verbal about our identity with the resurrected Christ. A fearful world needs a courageous church. We live in a fearful world. And yet there's an explosion of the gospel globally these days. We're living in a unique time in history. Each one of us has a part in that, no one is exempt. We have a mandate to share Jesus with everyone we can, which is one of the greatest joys we can experience. And we don't have to be a "super Christian" to do it. We're all in process, we're all under construction. Even the apostle Paul talked about his struggles in taking the gospel to the four corners of the globe. Here is what he wrote in 1 Corinthians 2:1-3; I think you can identify with what he's trying to communicate to you and me today.

> When I came to you, I did not come with eloquence or human wisdom as I proclaimed to you the testimony about God. For I resolved to know nothing while I was with you except Jesus Christ and him crucified. I came to you in weakness and great fear and trembling.

Paul? The apostle? He's our model and he struggled with those same things that you and I struggle with in relationship to living out the reality of Christ?

He continued, "My message and my preaching were not with wise and persuasive words, but were a demonstration of the Spirit's power, so that your faith might not rest on human wisdom, but on God's power" (2:4).

Fearful, but we power on.

One story that has always captivated me is John Bunyan's

Pilgrim's Progress. John Bunyan was in prison for twelve years for speaking about Jesus. After he was arrested, he could have been released had he promised never again to speak of Jesus publicly. But he refused. He had a wife and four kids, one of them blind. But he remained in prison for twelve years with his wife's blessings. "Don't retreat, Sweetheart," was her message to him. God did not waste those twelve years as John Bunyan was honoring Him. When John was released, he wrote *Pilgrim's Progress*, which is still the most famous Christian book in existence today.

Consider Dietrich Bonhoeffer, a pastor who lived under the Nazi regime. When other pastors were succumbing to the threats the German government made about sharing the truth of Jesus Christ, Bonhoeffer didn't back down. He ended up in jail because of it, but he stood true for Jesus. He said, "Not to speak is to speak. Not to act is to act."[1] If there was ever a need today, we need to trade up and ask God to give us a fresh dose of Christlike courage, no matter what the cost might be.

All you and I have is today. Yesterday is history, tomorrow's a mystery. We must not postpone obedience. When we feel the Spirit of God moving us in a certain direction, we must be careful not to say, "I'm going to do that, but I've got to get this other thing done before I can step out and do that thing."

God is clear that we must act, that the Christian life is to be lived by faith. We know Hebrews 11:6, which tells us, "Without faith it is impossible to please God." We cannot live by faith if we do not have the courage to fail. We cannot live by faith in what God asks of us unless we're willing to take risks. We cannot play it safe. The world is depending on us, so we need to come out of hiding with the message of the redeeming love of Jesus Christ.

Everything God asks us to do *today* has as its motivation, *that* day. You know what's going to take place on that day? Every knee is going to bow, every tongue is going to confess that Jesus Christ is Lord to the glory of the Father.

I've got a part and I need to play my "bit part." You have a part and you need to play your "bit part." And the "bit part" doesn't start tomorrow, it starts today. Why? Because I know that "'no eye has seen . . . no ear has heard, and . . . no human mind has conceived'—the things God has prepared for those who love him" (1 Corinthians 2:9).

Richard Halverson, longtime Senate chaplain, said this: "You go nowhere by accident. Wherever you go, God is sending you there. Wherever you are, God has put you there. He has purpose in your being there. Christ who indwells you has something He wants to do through you wherever you are."[2]

Believe this and go in His grace, His love, and His power. Jesus told us, "I am with you. Trust Me." So go public with Jesus. Find out what God has burning in the world and go pour the fuel on the fire and let God do His work. Go for broke. Go all in.

A CLOSING ADMONITION

John Maisel has lived his life exactly as he spoke of above. Over and over he has put everything on the line, has been all in for Jesus. We have much to learn from his life.

As Paul told us to follow him as he followed Christ, we can follow John's example as he too followed Christ. And as he passes the baton to the next generation, we have a great opportunity to grab it and run hard, giving it our all—so the world, in the darkest places, can hear of and know the Good News of the gospel of Jesus Christ.

What do you say? Will you be all in too?

A Prayer

Throughout this book we've learned from and celebrated the life and legacy of John Maisel. It seems fitting to have him close our time together in prayer.

Holy Father,

Thank You that we have been called to live in a time such as this. Thank You for Your presence that is within those who have said yes to the Lord Jesus.

I pray, Father, that in some way, just as You commanded Joshua to "be strong and courageous," You will bring that fresh and renewing message to the church in America today.

I pray that Your church will be strong in her identity and the indwelling presence of Jesus Christ. You have promised, "I will never leave you and I will never forsake you." May our strength be in our identity of Your indwelling presence. As a result of that, Father, would you infuse us to take our conviction of who You are and our walk with You and raise it to the level that we will become verbal and break this epidemic of silence that we find in the church in America today?

It is Your Spirit who ravished the heart of the first-century Christians. We pray and we ask in the name of Jesus Christ that Your Spirit would begin to ravish our hearts, convict us of our sin, and use us in the arenas that each Christian has been placed to publicly identify and willingly lose their life for Jesus' namesake, and for the sake of the gospel.

I pray that each one who reads this prayer will step forward and say, "I don't know what my part is, but with Your presence, may I courageously begin to go public in my identity with Jesus." I pray that Your redeeming love one day will go to every tribe and every tongue and every nation.

I pray this in the name of our Savior and for the glory of our Father and the joy of our soon-coming King. In the name above all names—Jesus. Amen.

AFTERWORD

My greatest privilege over the past twenty-seven years of international ministry has been to share the yoke and mantle of leadership with John Maisel. I worked first with John as a colleague for five years, then he was my "boss" for the next fourteen years. Finally these past eight years I am serving as his successor in leadership at East-West Ministries.

About seven years ago our leadership team at East-West rewrote the "core values" for the ministry. After a few days of prayerful deliberation, we landed on four new core values:

- A passion for Jesus
- A passion for grace
- A passion for the spiritually darkest places
- A passion for bold action

It was no surprise to me—or to our entire leadership team and board—that these four values epitomize John Maisel.

What makes John a great man, a great leader, a great evangelist, and a great world changer is the simple fact that he is completely sold out, surrendered, submitted, and obedient to Jesus Christ.

Period!

Jesus is the One who ravished John's heart when John was a very young man. Jesus still ravishes John's heart today and will ravish his heart every single day of the rest of his life. Put simply, John's life and legacy are the product of his unwavering, undiminished, and unfinished sixty-year love affair with Jesus.

As a result, John is laser focused on serving and glorifying his one and only King, Jesus Christ. John "lives and dies" every single day for the glory of God and for the advancement of God's eternal Kingdom. He patiently serves Jesus and awaits the eternal weight of glory for which he has been bought with a price by Jesus Christ in order to serve Him for all eternity.

Do you aspire to be a great man or woman of God, a great leader, a great soul winner, and a great world changer?

The thrilling good news that John would have you embrace as you close the final pages of this book is this: you can be! Greatness is not about who you are, it is about Whom you follow. The apostle Paul said, "Follow me as I follow Jesus." John Maisel can easily say the same.

What would John want you to take away from this book and from a brief reflection upon his life? Simply that he is a normal, broken human being who has been eternally captured and transformed by his marvelous Savior, Jesus Christ the Lord.

So how do we follow John as he follows Jesus?

By pursuing daily intimacy with Jesus and with His Word, the holy Scriptures. These are the lynchpin of John's life and legacy. John often exhorts those around him with these words:

Go deep with Jesus personally.
Walk with Jesus privately.
Make much of Jesus publicly.

And he constantly reminds us of the need to rest in Jesus' immeasurable grace. He says, "If there is no grace, there is no Maisel!" John encourages the application of God's immeasurable grace to his own heart and to our own shortcomings and failures with another exhortation when he states:

We are all in process.
We are all under construction.
None of us has arrived.
Be sure you cross the finish line with Jesus!

In this book's foreword, Jim Denison compared John to the apostle Paul, who near the end of his life wrote these sober and celebratory words: "I am already being poured out like a drink offering, and the time for my departure is near. I have fought the good fight, I have finished the race, I have kept the faith. Now there is in store for me the crown of righteousness, which the Lord, the righteous Judge, will award me on that day" (2 Timothy 4:6-8).

After reading this passage recently, John reflected upon his own life in light of Paul's words and he said, "There are three things I hope I'll have done at the end of my life: fought the fight, finished the race, kept the faith."

Jim Denison closed his foreword by encouraging us, "Now it's our turn."

Indeed, it is!

As John Maisel prepares to finish his final leg of the race with abundant faithfulness and fruitfulness and prepares to enter the "great cloud of witnesses" that the writer of Hebrews refers to, John's greatest passion is that you and I and the next generation will take that baton from his hand and *run*.

I pray that you may run after Jesus and run for the glory of His eternal Kingdom in such a way that you may win. And Hebrews 12 continues, "Let us throw off everything that hinders and the sin that so easily entangles. And let us run with perseverance the race marked out for us, fixing our eyes on Jesus, the pioneer and perfecter of faith. For the joy set before him he endured the cross, scorning its shame, and sat down at the right hand of the throne of God. Consider him who endured such opposition from sinners, so that you will not grow weary and lose heart" (12:1-4).

Godspeed as you follow Jesus and Paul and countless others—and fix your eyes on Jesus as John has done so well—and run the race marked out in front of you to the glory of Jesus Christ. Amen!

—Kurt Nelson

President and CEO, East-West Ministries

ACKNOWLEDGMENTS

I want to acknowledge the gift of friendship that John Maisel has extended to me these past several years. He has modeled to me personally everything that has been described about him in this simple biography.

Many thanks to Ginger Kolbaba for her tremendous editing skills, writing skills, and spirit of generosity that made this publication possible.

Many thanks to Kurt Nelson and Kristen Schuler at East-West who provided important direction of this book. Kristen provided the photographs for this publication.

Many thanks to the team who has helped to produce this book—David Sluka, Katherine Lloyd, Yvonne Parks, Christy Distler, and the Mattera Management Team. Your skills are amazing, and we are so indebted to you.

Many thanks to the friends who believed in and supported this project.

Many thanks to the Christian community in Greater Dallas, which has really been the "Antioch of America" with such extraordinary leadership and generosity. Your model is changing the world daily.

ABOUT THE AUTHOR

Mac Pier is founder and CEO of Movement.Org. He also serves as the Lausanne Global Catalyst for Cities. He has authored seven books, including *A Disruptive Gospel* and *A Disruptive God*. In 2018, *Outreach* magazine named *A Disruptive Gospel* an Outreach Resource of the Year.

In 2016, Mac directed Movement Day Global Cities in New York City for three thousand leaders and four hundred cities from ninety-five nations, and in 2018 directed the One Hundred Cities Summit in Washington DC.

Mac has been married to Marya for nearly forty years. They have three married adult children and four grandchildren. They have lived in New York City for thirty-five years.

NOTES

Foreword

1 "Evangelism Statistics," Bible.org, https://bible.org/illustration
   /evangelism-statistics, accessed December 13, 2018.
2 "51% of Churchgoers Don't Know of the Great Commission," Barna,
   March 27, 2018, https://www.barna.com/research/half-churchgoers
   -not-heard-great-commission/, accessed December 13, 2018.
3 George Barna, "Survey: Christians Are Not Spreading the Gospel,"
   November 30, 2017, http://www.georgebarna.com/research-flow
   /2017/11/30/survey-christians-are-not-spreading-the-gospel,
   accessed December 13, 2018.

Chapter 1: Meeting John Maisel

1 Movement Day convenes diverse faith leaders from the same city
   to tackle spiritual and social issues. Our team has convened twenty
   thousand leaders from four hundred cities and ninety-five countries
   to catalyze gospel movements in cities.

   In its first five years, Movement Day DFW has convened six
   thousand leaders from more than three hundred churches. In its
   first 2014 gathering in Dallas, 1,400 leaders convened at the Kay
   Bailey Hutchinson Convention Center. Some said it was the most
   significant gathering of Dallas faith leaders people had seen in their
   lifetime.
2 East-West's vision and mission statements, taken from their ministry site at www.eastwest.org/what-we-do/.
3 John has continued as a board member for Explore God in addition
   to his president emeritus status of East-West, where he still focuses
   most of his time and energy.

4 N. T. Wright, *Paul: A Biography* (New York: Harper Collins, 2018), 52.

Chapter 2: A Man's Man

1 "President John F. Kennedy's Inaugural Address (1961)," https://www.ourdocuments.gov/doc.php?flash=false&doc=91&page=transcript%20.

Chapter 3: The Road to Moscow

1 Tarkan Rosenberg, "The Downfall of Communism," Thoughtco.com, August 17, 2018, https://www.thoughtco.com/the-downfall-of-communism-1779970.
2 N. T. Wright, *Paul: A Biography*, 22.
3 Stephen Um and Justin Buzzard, *Why Cities Matter* (Wheaton, IL: Crossway, 2013), 123.
4 The Iron Curtain represented all of the nations that were dominated by communism. These would include the forty nations mentioned earlier in the chapter.

Chapter 4: Two Speeches at Moscow State University

1 Bret Baier, *Three Days in Moscow* (New York: William Morrow Pub, 2018), 141–142.
2 Ibid., 152.
3 Ibid., 152.
4 Ronald Reagan, Moscow State University Address, May 31, 1988, American Rhetoric Online Speech Bank, https://www.americanrhetoric.com/speeches/ronaldreaganmoscowstateuniversity.htm.
5 Excerpted from John's speech with his permission. Much of what John shared during his speech can also be found in his booklet *Is Jesus God?* published by East-West Ministries. To receive a copy of *Is Jesus God?* please contact East-West Ministries at 1-972-941-4500 or 2001 West Plano Parkway, Suite 3000, Plano, TX 75075.
6 C. S. Lewis, *Mere Christianity* (San Francisco: HarperOne, 1952, 1980), 52.

Chapter 5: From Moscow to the World

1 To learn more about East-West's current initiatives or to get involved with Great Commission work through East-West, visit www.eastwest .org.

2 The Global Day of Prayer, "History," http://www.globaldayofprayer .com/wp-content/uploads/1.-History-20141.pdf.

3 J. I. Packer, *Knowing God* (Downers Grove, IL: InterVarsity, 1973), 30–32.

Chapter 7: Take a Stand—No Matter What

1 Mircea Pacurariu, "Romanian Christianity," in Ken Parry, *The Blackwell Companion to Eastern Christianity* (Hoboken, NJ: Blackwell, 2007), 293, 297.

Chapter 8: The Courage to Go Public

1 Josh Crossman, "Episode 15—Josh Crossman, The Great Opportunity, Tripling Church Planting," Send Institute, May 28, 2018, https://www.sendinstitute.org/podcast-episode/episode-15 -josh-crossman-great-opportunity-tripling-church-planting/.

2 Ron Owens, *They Could Not Stop the Music* (Collierville, TN: Innovo Publishing, 2016), 88–89.

Chapter 10: Looking Toward the Future

1 Eric Metaxas, *Bonhoeffer Study Guide: The Life and Writings of Dietrich Bonhoeffer* (Nashville, TN: Thomas Nelson, 2014), 59.

2 The Pastor's Workshop, "Benedictions," http://thepastorsworkshop .com/liturgy/benedictions/.